Memo for a Movie

A Short Life of Dietrich Bonhoeffer

Theodore A. Gill

THE MACMILLAN COMPANY
NEW YORK, NEW YORK

For the colleagues—
Adele, George,
Ralph, Tom,
cheerleaders and slave drivers—
and
Lillian,
who produced the producer

Copyright © 1971 by Green Gill Productions

All rights reserved. No part of this book may be reproduced or transmitted in any form or by any means, electronic or mechanical, including photocopying, recording or by any information storage and retrieval system, without permission in writing from the Publisher.

The Macmillan Company
866 Third Avenue, New York, N.Y. 10022
Collier-Macmillan Canada Ltd., Toronto, Ontario

Library of Congress Catalog Card Number: 71–80301

FIRST MACMILLAN PAPERBACKS EDITION 1971

Printed in the United States of America

CONTENTS

CONTENTS

Introduction

TO WHATEVER AUDIENCE

What follows is exactly what it purports to be: a memo, a notation of the narrative facts and interpretive possibilities for a projected film on Dietrich Bonhoeffer. A memo is not a screenplay, not a scenario, not a "treatment." Certainly not this memo, anyway. Any movie filmed directly from the following pages would play at least forty-nine hours—forty-nine rambling uncinematic, inartistic hours. Selection, compression will have to come next when a story line strong as a purse string pulls tight what necessarily sprawls and gaps in a preliminary documentation. Meanwhile, a quasi-cinematic form is used for the memo, more to keep both author and reader aware of the occasion for this compiling than to give film technicians cues in a business they know best.

Such a memo is a factual work of the imagination. It is factual because the main characters, the main events, were as met here. Most of the facts are certifiable in these pages because they were previously certified in private conversations or on other pages by many of the actors in the story—relatives, students, colleagues, friends—and especially by Eberhard Bethge, who from inside his various studies of Dietrich Bonhoeffer will call out the principal facts to researchers in all the generations left.

But the ensuing sketch is a work of the imagination too. A memo for a movie is not a scientific biography—whatever that might be. It is a selection and arrangement of facts which the arranger believes tell an arresting and important story, which story the writer's information, intuitions, and imagination tell him is the true story. So, as conscious of his meanings as of his medium, the memo-maker's informed imagination moves through the available material, selecting this event and discarding that, emphasizing this person and passing by that, filling out this event and skimping that. To make conceptual points in narrative ways, occasionally minor characters have to be developed more confidently than the records would really sustain. To obviate a cliché "cast of thousands," a composite figure may have to be made occasionally of several separately important persons. The few conversations indicated hereafter will finally have to be contrived from almost whole cloth. All such adjustments are justified within the film treatment, of course, only if they present truly the certifiable point being made.

Any movie developed from this memo will continue to depend upon such imagination. Writers, producers, directors, above all, the acting artists will have to use their imaginations throughout: for hunches on motivation, for guesses at atmosphere, for intuitions of the untold, for the perception of a design in the welter of events. The largest truth always depends on the imagination. Such imaginative extensions as are in this memo are hazarded on the strength of facts that belong to our own history.

ﷺ

TO THE MOVIE MAKERS

Gore Vidal somewhere distinguishes Scott Fitzgerald from many of his writing successors by noting Fitzerald's careful search for "the right word and the relevant incident." For the present project the right words will depend upon the right screen-writer and the right producer and the right director and the right stars—both kinds. The shooting script which you artist-professionals finally agree on will, it is hoped, meld right words and relevant incident.

Meanwhile, here are amassed the narrative data. They include, most obviously, the dramatic facts of Dietrich Bonhoeffer's unlikely life. A child of plenty, personable, brilliant, many-talented, develops sweetly in his family privilege. He travels, he plays, he excels at the university, he enters the Lutheran ministry. He proclaims a solidly biblical gospel and enforces a traditional piety. He honors the government, preaches no politics, exalts the church, considers pacifism. He gets a great kick out of being around. Then his nation accepts a mad suitor, the atmosphere is suddenly electric with threat, Bonhoeffer goes into the Resistance. At home he opposes, abroad he exposes the lie of his government and too many of its people. On the move or hiding out, he writes, preaches, teaches, exhorts, schemes. He refuses safety, operates as a kind of double agent in his own country and a courier to the enemy, enters a conspiracy against the life of the head of state, is misunderstood by the church, betrayed by colleagues, imprisoned, hanged, burned to lost ashes in the Nazi ovens. Years after the war, a friend collects and publishes letters and poems written by Bonhoeffer from prison. Realistic young students find in these fragments more suggestion for twentieth-century faith and life than in any of their other teachers, and the fascination and fame of Dietrich Bonhoeffer begins its enormous spread and usefulness.

The story is worth filming on its own account. A complex hero is swept into historic events and the scenerio quite honestly explodes into razzle-dazzle, hanky-panky, and derring-do with a real martyrdom for toppers. Such an account of personal development in the midst of earth-shaking, earth-shattering events, all true, will spark dramatic treatment in all media in all time ahead.

But the present treatment is interested in more than the principle character and his tempestuous times. It is as much interested in us and our own threatening period. And because Bonhoeffer's time was the upbeat for that whole discordant era in which we still flounder, we need take no liberties with his story to make it antiphon to ours. If we tell his story straight it might help us see around some of our own blind corners. We do not try here to learn from his history so we will not have to repeat it; we *are* repeating it, it is all our history.

Do we film the 1930s or the 1960s when we show a man exposing the criminal potentiality in a conservatism that would clamp the lid on the *status quo* while a changing, churning history underneath the artificial order hastens the awful explosion such sealed conservatism ensures? Is it then or now when a desperate patriot decries the worked-out weariness of a once-lively liberalism? Where are the intervening decades when a youth denounces the blood mysticism of the radicals, that maddening, sense-less assumption of idealistic demagogues that right-eousness will come automatically when the right righteous are in, that the empowered "folk" will nat-urally make things right? Is it history we hear or history we are caught in when the script takes up the earlier debate on law and order, racism, dissent, militarism? And what about our hero's struggle with issues of resistance, violence and nonviolence, assassination: how *déjà vu* can you be?

By being himself, in his own time, Dietrich Bon-hoeffer is a bomb under all the standard positions of contemporaneity on all our continuing problems. For instance, if you introduce him right he will represent all the good, solid, respectable people of the century we share. None should have trouble recognizing him as the best of that estimable crowd. But then Bonhoeffer explodes in their midst. Exact-ly because he takes seriously the theological and his-torical bases of Western religion and respectability, he cannot abide the vulgar horror that the conven-tionally righteous are letting this culture become. This is one position he demolishes from the inside, with its own weapons. For profoundly conservative reasons, he goes into the resistance. His story con-demns every sit-tight, stand-pat good man.

But only and always for effectiveness, never for effect. Just as Bonhoeffer's life and death condemn every easy alliance with things as they are, so do they condemn every resistance given to gestures. Bonhoeffer, already a hero on many of our cam-puses, will surprise some of his noisier devotees if you can show him in his own truth. He never wasted a minute of his time nor an erg of his energy putting himself in the right light (except to confound his captors). He schemed always for the main chance, cared little for the appearance of radical purity or modish righteousness. He was deeply offended by look-at-me screamers, no matter how right their causes. Resistance was not an end in itself, ever; it was the only way from here to there so he took it, but he wanted to get there as quickly as possible. Neither did revolutionary enthusiasm ever make him contemptuous of living. At the end he fought by every legal stratagem to stay alive. Grandiloquence was to him a trivialization of the issue. And he never countenanced limiting resistance to only one strategy or weapon from that whole armamentorium of possibilities on which he continuously drew.

To some of us he says "Get going"; to others, "Get smart." And for none has he ease.

There are still other reasons for this cinematic look at Dietrich Bonhoeffer. The film envisioned will have missed an important part of the mark if, beside being a good story and a more than oblique comment on current public issues, it is not also the exploration of a currently viable sanctity.

Just as you would have to redefine martyrdom to make Bonhoeffer a martyr, so you would have to redefine sanctity to make him a saint. But that latter would be a worthwhile effort if it were un-

7

dertaken, not to give Bonhoeffer extra credit but to rehabilitate, perhaps, the notion that some kind of holiness has some place in our profane world. Bonhoeffer's usefulness toward such a reclamation is *not* in his occasional somewhat strained efforts after a conventionally recognizable sanctity. These enterprises in tradition sat awkwardly on him, ring hollow with us. It is rather when least interested in questions of sanctity, most absorbed in being wholly, intensely human, that he is most interesting as an illustration of what a twentieth-century, sophisticated, knowing, sensual, man of the world saint might be—a man that our knowledgeable contemporaries might conceivably find admirable and even worth emulating today (if saints have any residual function, surely it is as possible model?).

So the memo anticipates, exhorts a movie that celebrates in Dietrich Bonhoeffer a man for *our* seasons, a man between the times, between the worlds, between the certainties, between the culture's phases. Where a Thomas More put aside some human claims to die for a principle, Dietrich Bonhoeffer put aside several dear principles before he died himself, making a claim for humanity. And that may be the difference between the sixteenth and the twentieth centuries and their sanctities.

Writing afterwards, the Bishop of Chichester said, "Dietrich himself was a martyr many times before he died." Since the tender English bishop was a kind of father confessor to the young German, it may be that part of his reference was to some sacrifice of private interest known only to him. But there is no need to go imagining beyond Bonhoeffer's very public record to find numerous convictional martyrdoms, the repeated *throwing in* of whatever, however precious to him, obstructed his designated service of man.

It must be made obvious in the film, for instance, that between the beginning and the close, Bonhoeffer throws in the privileges and pleasures of the comfortable life of an intellectual, an aesthete, to end as a convict, a brutalized victim, a naked corpse charred to scattered ashes. A true script will have to find early ways to italicize Bonhoeffer's affection for the world and its culture, his joy in his own life and strength and style, and all of this all the way to the empty end. He gives up what he has to, but he never makes things easier for himself by inducing a contempt for what he can't have anyway (as earlier, more diaphanous saints might have: dogs in the manger, inside out). Bonhoeffer's world was never dearer to him than when he threw it in, and the longer he was away from it, the higher its commonest aspects moved in his most serious values.

Bonhoeffer was a proud German who spent his last years praying that Germany would be defeated, and doing what he could to insure that humiliation.

Bonhoeffer was a universal man, at least an international man, at home in the whole world. He gloried in his freedom to identify with everyone everywhere. To turn his back on all that as he did, voluntarily closing himself again into one sick nation, one tormented people, one tight, sealed, hated state was another of those preliminary, deliberate martyrdoms for this inquisitive, appreciative man of the whole world.

But it wasn't just his internationalism that Bonhoeffer threw in when he returned to Germany and to peril. He was one of the earliest, youngest, most ardent ecumenical statesmen, moving between the churches, seeking to adjust differences. It was ecumenical agencies and leaders who arranged the chance for him to serve this ideal abroad when danger threatened him at home. When he rejected that offer, it was more than a return to danger that troubled. For he was also abandoning (or, at least, setting aside) another commitment. He did not just return to Germany; he returned to keep divided one ailing church even though he was sure there was no health for any church till the divisions between all the churches were healed.

Most dramatic of all these sacrifices, of course, was the immurement of his pacifistic instincts. How close he finally came to a Gandhian ideal, under profoundly biblical pressures, will have to be made clear in the film. It is to be hoped that this subtle point can be made positively enough so that the terrible wrench is felt by all when he gives up his third attempt to visit Gandhi in India, in order to return home where he is shortly involved in the plotting against Hitler. And that plotting, for the pacific young pastor, was never limited to nonviolence. Others might hope to jail or hospitalize the dictator; Bonhoeffer never doubted that anti-Christ had to be removed and was willing to play his part and to share the guilt for *whatever* was necessary to destroy Hitler. Bonhoeffer's strategic certainty is clear; the personal agony on his way to it, unfathomable. His colleagues in the conspiracy plotted too, but their plotting was more of a piece with their fine, generous, humane instincts. Bonhoeffer shared all those, but he also had a sweet ideal that he had to jettison in order to give scope to those instincts and the murderous contrivance that they finally arrive at.

Other convictions, if not exactly thrown in, yielded too. The church, once seen by Bonhoeffer as almost vis-à-vis the world, came to be seen as faithful only when it was joining the world, getting into the world, throwing itself away on the world. Jesus Christ, once analyzed by Bonhoeffer with enormous theological sophistication in his metaphysical being and cosmological significance, by the end of the young professor's life was being hailed as "the man for others," almost as if that were enough for the Christian's public claim about Him. The striking theological interpretations and biblical studies with which Bonhoeffer had established his early international fame by the time he wrote his prison letters were somehow in question (to the continuing consternation of those who still hail more confidently his safer beginnings). At the end, Bonhoeffer was reaching for ways to talk about man and his hope without invoking the word "God" at all—yet never himself stopped saying "God." In the name of Christ, he protested religion and "religious" language—yet took comfort to the end in the phrases of traditional devotion. And an ethics, which through most of his professional life he tried to give some structured order, he at last directed toward the most and best that any man could realize, he being who he is, reality being what it is, the situation being what it is, the possibilities being what they are.

American film makers, because this whole development of thought is so congenial to their own, may miss the poignancy in Bonhoeffer's theological pilgrimage. He was a European whose lofty essay after his first stay in the United States contrasted American to European theology, *not* to the Americans' advantage. Yet this proud German theologian, had he lived to sum up his own development to 1945, might have observed that the definition of religion he had come to by then was at least as much at home in that American tradition for which he had little respect as it was in the European tradition which he had exemplified among us and in which he lived most easily. He was a classicist, and before he winds up he is also a subtle but practical liberal looking for what works. And if those final developments meant house arrest for some Very Important Traditions, then he was ready to arrange a secret place for that (where he would himself still honor the traditions). This was a man of notable rectitude, and he turned out all sinuosity on ethical issues.

These late developments in Bonhoeffer's thought became the beginnings of much contemporary religious thought. For them he is honored. But for Bonhoeffer himself the second look at certainties, the questioning of directions, the venturing into he knew-not-what just when his physical existence was most imperiled, was as desolating as it was daring.

You who make the movie cannot be faulted if you do not get all this in! But the responsible artists may be helped by such interpretation to give dimension and texture to the characterization. *Some* of this must get in explicity, though, so viewers will really know how much is happening when it finally happens, how much more than just another life is lost.

Dietrich Bonhoeffer's story is not merely the latest listing in humanity's record of occasional, fatal valiance. What makes his end worth turning the lights on it are all the intermediate endings. So many other even more significant deaths are sealed in that final one. So much else was given up before life was given up, so much else was taken before life was taken.

Too many meanings have already been posted here to ride on the backs of events that will probably run only ninety minutes. And if the number of meanings didn't intimidate, then their variety would. What would seem to be needed is some sense of single drive which would organize the scattered significances in an order that has some congruity with the picturable people and events. And there is such an organizing principle, I think (impersonality must be abandoned in this section, for here I hazard entirely personal interpretations; T.A.G.). The trouble with finding it is that the possibility is lodged in the heart of a dense theology, and it will be hard to effect transparence with a new opacity. But I must try.

Bonhoeffer-interpretation is by now in a deep purple embarrassment of riches. If we try here for our own interpretation, it is not at all because there are no learned guides; it is because there are so many, and all are formidably authoritative, so how to choose?

Peter Vorkink II aptly refers to Bonhoeffer interpretation today as a kind of theological Rorschach, with the various scholars announcing what pictures they see in the conceptual shapes left in such enigmatic profusion by Bonhoeffer. Some make order by counting out all the late, more radical utterances. Karl Barth, for instance, is said to have limited his students' thesis work on Bonhoeffer to the writing before 1939—that is, to the more or less obediently Barthian early work, and you can't get much more magisterial than that in modern Protestantism.

Others, just as determined to restore familiar form to the young theologian whom they fear came somewhat unraveled at the end, insist on interpreting all the exciting last notes in terms of the familiar, fashionable, utterly unexceptionable writing that went first. Such interpreters are, of course, themselves very fashionable now. It is exceedingly modish these days to press whatever is popularly taken as new, back under the blanket of the old. Historical studies are whirling lathes in which all the corners and bumps of novelty are rounded into similarity. We are reminded regularly how fundamentally Jewish Jesus was, how truly medieval (when you get right down to it) Luther and Calvin were, how of-a-Christocentric-piece Bonhoeffer was even when he went antireligious.

This historical approach is an important one, of course, essential, true. It is smart with the professionals at the moment, and can remain so if it doesn't go smart-aleck too often. Reading the end from the beginning is all right as far as it goes, if it doesn't go all the way. For when it goes all the way that is reductionism, which must be denied the humane historians just as strenuously as they deny reductionism to the physical and behaviorial scientists. It is certainly no service to Bonhoeffer nor any use to us to explain his most arresting suggestions in such a way as to explain them away. The Bonhoeffer left when some of his analysts get through with him is no one anyone would ever have looked at twice, much less developed an international furor over. They explain everything but the fuss. If that is indeed their pleasure, we must leave it at that: Even Bonhoeffer insisted that such secrets of motivation need be confessed to only one other person. Anyway, if Bonhoeffer's last writings are only incautious adjustments of his first, there is that much less reason for filming the story of one who is then a brisk but secondary figure in Christian letters, tinkering with a voguish theology already on its way out.

The Roman Catholic commentators find Bonhoeffer a *smörgåsbord* of agreeable possibilities. The more traditional note his liturgical sympathies, his youthful empathies in Rome, his subsequent quasimonasticisms, his satisfaction in the Luther-authorized sign of the cross, and his mature attachment to the *Klöster* at Ettal. More liberal Catholics of course rejoice in his biblicism: finally learning to return to the Bible themselves, they delight to find him standing beside their revered Barth when they get to that strange new world. And his doctrine of transubstantiation, though with him it is the church rather than just the sacramental elements that becomes the very body of Christ, is friendly. For the radicals, he is brother and teacher as he is for Protestant and Jewish radicals, too. And don't try to tell them that he didn't take a quite new look at things from his several prisons. Put all the Roman Catholics together and you get approbation of almost all of Bonhoeffer, then—which doesn't help much when we're trying to discriminate an organizing element.

The East Europeans, in this as in so much else, reverse the West Europeans' judgment. Instead of the beginnings controlling the end, East Germans find the end giving the beginnings the only importance they may have. After all of Bonhoeffer's earlier talk about the West and Christendom somehow being special concretions of divine will and favor, deserving our defense, it is his apparent abandonment of all such thought, his final openness to the future come what may, his hailing of novelty in human relations and institutions in a world come of age, his nonreligious interpretation of the gospel in friendly address to atheist self-sufficiency—these are the call letters that keep Eastern Europeans tuned in to Bonhoeffer. But such a simple change of mind, such a flip-flop (*if* it could be proven), would hardly be the stuff of drama.

Eberhard Bethge gives the best clue to what we seek. And the clue this intimate of Bonhoeffer offers is not so much a common theme or dominant idea or even a *Leitmotiv*, as it is a personal manner, method, style, drive of the man, Dietrich Bonhoeffer. What Bethge singles out as giving coherence to a life of reflection *in which there were real developments*, is "concreteness." From the beginning to end, while the mind changed, its bent to presentness and practicality never relaxed. A cosmic windiness like "transcendence," for instance, is not for Bonhoeffer an ontological separateness that must be proven about God; it is a primary fact that proves itself every time you meet another person or consider another's good. The adult Bonhoeffer could not think of God as Something or Someone Over There. The only God he was willing to talk about was the one who shows up in Jesus Christ—and the Jesus Christ he prefers is not a memory or an exalted vision but is the church. And the church he means is not a drafty ideal in which an ectoplasmic Christ makes His airy home but is a present congregation—and that congregation not in contemplation but in action, the pulpit taking chances, the people getting busy. Faith is never just a nod of the mind, but is an act of the whole man; it is obedience—physical, historical, objective obedience. Confession is not something you syllabilize aiming your mouth at heaven, nor is forgiveness an ineffable that wafts down from the sky. Confession is something you admit to one other person and forgiveness is the assurance he offers you.

The list could be extended. Wherever you touch Bonhoeffer he is talking about us, what we're up against, here and now. Concreteness is not one of the themes of his theology, it is the key the whole work is written in.

Which means that even in the problematic heart of his theological writings, Dietrich Bonhoeffer is made for the movies! Ideas are not necessarily photogenic and theological development is not immediately cinematic. But with Bonhoeffer that doesn't matter. The point of all his teaching is there, in the concreteness—the graspable detail, the tellable event, the picturability—of his existence and ours.

With no person in the history of ideas is it less likely that a disengaged mind seized an abstract idea and disinterestedly tracked through its implications. No mind ever really has operated as aseptically; how could it, considering the basic stuffiness of spirit? With Dietrich Bonhoeffer, as with *everyone* else, there is a personal predisposition (the genetically given), and there are the accidents of encounter (with men, ideas—including the religious—places, events), and there is the person's specific intelligence, analyzing the options presented by the encounters, choosing a stance, finding equilibrium for himself and justifying it to a world open to various interpretations. He locates ideas that explain himself, give him some use, interpret the word *he* lives in (inside and out). And if he is a theologian he teaches these ideas. Every theology is its writer's *apologia pro vita sua*.

Bonhoeffer's theological concreteness is of a piece with his native enthusiasm about things and stuff. Even the word "concrete" is too abstract for the fact. He was good at living, knew it, and rejoiced in it. No record or book will ever have the whole story of all the familial, physical affirmations his thinking emerged from. That is part of his fascination: the sense of between-the-lines affections, loyalties, engrossments, adventures, all of which involved as much of him in as much of the world as he could get next to.

If a traditional stage piece were being attempted here, the facts lend themselves handily to the old pattern. Act I sets the happy scene; Act II introduces the complication that deflects the natural development of bliss (the eternal *duo* ramifies into a pro tem triangle); Act III sees adjustments and/or restorations.

So, after opening scenes established Bonhoeffer in his close alliance with people, world, flesh, family, art, the middle scenes would be concerned with the complications that ensue when relic pieties and influential new teachers persuade him to put Last Things first, to subordinate this world to the Other, to let distance mute both satisfactions and expectations by looking at them all *sub specie aeternitatis*.

This second act is complicated the more by having a beloved part of his world slap at him in its political developments while his exalted church disappoints and fails him in the main. He is momentarily thrown off stride, which does not mean that his development is arrested or altered but only that for a time the pace is changed. A quasi-monastic interlude at this point is not the "detour" it has been called, but is a tunnel: walls closed in, but rails still going directly ahead, and light coming closer at the end.

In Act III he breaks out of the tunnel. He is back in rangy action, he recovers joy. Circumstances are by now not just threatening but desperate. Yet it is while he is in real danger, on the run, that he shows himself full of an excited affirmation of the very life and world in which he was currently imperiled. All the earlier theological writing is seen now as his Czerny études—finger exercises—getting him ready for the main compositions to come. Unhappily, after all that practice, there is just time for him to announce principle themes, but it is obvious from them that the solo performance is beginning. Only now does his tone clear; somehow he gets out of his own way and disposes his models instead of being disposed by them. In the conspiracy and in prison he suddenly grows up, becomes the Bonhoeffer who matters to us, isolates and italicizes some of his own earlier leads; shouts back to us that it is this world and its people that the Other—if you *will* speak of it —is all about. In "a world come of age," increasingly competent, declaring its independence of mother church (long after cutting the umbilical cord, finally snapping the apron strings too), if meaning and hope are to be maintained at all then they must be located in people and events and things themselves, not in Places and People fancifully positioned on quaint, discredited maps. In the last scenes Bonhoeffer is finding the way to full, frank affirmation of the Act I life and world that he never wanted, understood, loved more than in the moment of his death. At the last curtain he is looking for better, newer theological ways to affirm what his person and career had affirmed vitally from the beginning. Only the terminal affirmation is more important than the temperamental one because it incorporates the whole Act II agony of testing and trying to understand. If, as some claim, Bonhoeffer comes out at last with a humanism, that is a *theological* humanism, an expensive humanism, not a cheap humanism. It is one which learns from theological analysis what human heights and depths must now be described and defended in other than religious terms.

And Bonhoeffer just had time to get started with that. *There* is the tragedy. To see his death only in connection with his politics is to rob it of stature. It has pathos and irony—he dies at the manic whim of the dying foe, with whose own end Bonhoeffer's death has nothing to do except for such satisfaction as it may have given the tyrant—but it does not have tragedy. The tragedy of his death lies in its irrelevance to the issues he was pressing at the end. He would much rather have *lived* them out. That had come to be the whole point.

During his involvement with the conspiracy (while keeping out of sight in the library of the Roman Catholic monastery at Ettal), Bonhoeffer wrote a chapter for his *Ethics* which he called "The Last Things and the Things Before the Last." My interpretation of Bonhoeffer has depended upon an expansion of the terms he uses there and an account of what became of them in his subsequent reflection. By "Last Things" (the Ultimate) he means in his essay God's forgiveness, acceptance, and eternal affirmation of men. By "the Things Before the Last" (the Penultimate) he means what men do or make to prepare for or to appropriate God's acceptance. It is perhaps not too violent an extension, then, to let the ultimate stand for God, His love, His judgments, His culminations and eternities, while the penultimate comprehends men, their ideals, religious life, friendships, culture, manners—the best of the fugitive human enterprise.

In these terms, Bonhoeffer began happily at home in the penultimate, cordially hailing the ultimate. In the course of his theological development, however, the entente came apart, and he agreed more and more with teachers who put a gulf between Ultimate and Penultimate, with all meaning, value, and hope Over There. He tries for a while, when the world goes bad around him, to give all his attention to the remote ultimate. He justifies his irrepressible interest in the things of the world for the chance it gives him to make these Penultimates serve the Ultimate. It is as if he hoped some of the significance of ultimacy might spill over onto the otherwise lightweight Penultimate if the latter could be made useful to the former.

But this interpretation didn't satisfy him long. It flew too obviously in the face of a native attachment to "the earth and its creatures" whose significance he *knew* was not borrowed, imported or derivative. So at the end of his life these Penultimates were more in the ascendancy than ever before.

In the prison letters it was as if he came home at last to his vital, vivid family and their passion for what is important here and now. But he brings with him rich treasure from his trip. He knows better than anyone *how* important their importants are, how much more they have done then they knew they were doing, what enormous meanings ride on the back of their spontaneous acts.

For the world, this life, each other—this is what we have to go on. He was realizing that the Ultimate is not seen, described, grasped, used, or served except in, with, under, via the Penultimate. So the ultimate doesn't just condescend to, it in some way *depends upon* the Penultimate. Instead of that earlier accommodation—the Penultimate borrowing its importance from whatever relation to the Ultimate it could claim—now the Ultimate in a way owes its very presence (and others will later say "existence") to the Penultimate.

Collating this whole latter discussion with the earlier bruited stage pattern yields this grotesque:

Act I.   Love affair with the Penultimate;

Act II.   Enchantment by the Ultimate;

Act III.   Back to the first love—to find the Other included there.

Actually, a pattern from quite another art fits Bonhoeffer's development better. As anybody who has attempted such an interpretation could report, too simple a linear development distorts even what it means to describe. For in an almost eerie way it is all there all the time: ends presaged in beginnings, beginnings showing themselves to the end, incessant back and forthings. Which is not to deny at last what was earlier insisted so strenuously, that there are real departures in the last prison hints and soundings. But it is to say that these novelties come when Bonhoeffer begins to see more than he had seen before in the possibilities of his original disposition and in his own earlier writing.

The best pattern comes from Bonhoeffer's favorite art, music. He develops in sonata form: first theme, second theme, development, recapitulation, coda. What was generally considered penultimacy, I say, is his main theme; traditional ultimacy is the second theme and in the development it is for a while dominant. But in the recapitulation the first theme is more important, interesting, reinforced, more richly *itself*, even in the unfinished movement we are left, than it was in its first innocent announcement. The continuously, marvelously contrapuntal development it went through with the second theme (in this pattern, both themes are present and interacting from beginning to end) gives its final restatement the power of new statement, ragged as its notation is.

There is, of course, no coda.

Opening
and Credits

UPBEAT

There is no music. Filling the half-lit screen, a strong hand, fingers clenching a broken, much-bitten pencil stub, swiftly, violently writing "Dietrich Bonhoeffer" on the fly leaf of a book. Immediately the signature is finished, the book is flung open to an inside page and the signature is repeated, slashed across the printed lines (as the camera pulls back slightly, the page heading identifies the book as a volume of Plutarch). The whole episode is only moments long. Force, haste is its keynote. The silence must scream of suppression: the sound the pencil makes, the sudden riffle of pages, the steady but strained breath of a man fighting terror, the impatient rustle of other men forced to wait while the horror of what they are about to do presses to be finished and the awful fascination of violent death allures.

For the firm hand is all through with pencils and words now. The men we sense but only now see as the scene widens are there to hang Dietrich Bonhoeffer. In ten minutes he will be dead. So might anyone, of course, but most would not know that, and no one who did could know it with the desolation in Bonhoeffer's knowledge: of his own gift for living, of his superb physical vitality and unique intellectual power, of brilliant ideas barely broached and waiting for his expansions, of the pathos in rescue then only a few miles from his prison, of the absurdity in a pointless death ordained by a defeated, already dying tyrant—of the infinite qualitative difference between being alive and being dead.

So the sounds are of controlled desperation, and the sight, too, as the whole man is seen now, closing the book, standing it prominently on a table, muttering to a troubled guard, "Eberhard, Maria, my family will wonder how far I got." Then, all brusque business, the guards hurry him out of the tiny room, down the narrow aisle running the

length of the block-long prison barracks, past the
blank doors still sealing condemned friends into
their final cells (but the last two doors already omi-
nously open on emptiness), and into the big, bare
room in the middle of the barracks. The outside
door is just closing behind a naked man, exiting between guards. The door is bolted, violently, metallic
rasping shredding further the tense composures in
the room. The guards order Bonhoeffer to strip. He
does so, deliberate, distant. Between his guards
again, he stands before the locked door. They wait.
A sharp rap from the outside, and the door is flung
open. Bonhoeffer steps into the bleak, high-walled
prison yard. The barracks itself is the wall behind
him. At the far ends of the barracks, short walls
meet the long featureless implacability of the opposite wall, beyond which the slave-labor camp lies
still in its silence of exhaustion.

It is spring dawn. Even here there is birdsong,
and over the walls to the right, treetops in new
green foliage; there is the new season's softness in
the air. But Bonhoeffer, who notes it all, who has
loved it all in the thirty-nine Aprils before, may not
linger now. The guards will not permit it; neither
will the young minister's pride, nor his faith, nor
the shock that mercifully shrouds such rare sensi-
tivities and imaginations in such extremity. He is
turned to his left. A gallows is terrible against the
blank end wall. The first sight of the noose tears
through even the shock for a moment: "God" is the
gasp. He walks to his waiting executioners.

Deep calm in the youthful scholar, nude at the

foot of the stairs now. He is positioned biblically: how could he not have remembered Job's "naked came I out of my mother's womb, and naked shall I return hither."* It is not a moment for amusement, but there is wryness in the wish to smile with a friend at this Old Testament predicament in these Bavarian woods. So in absolute silence (let nature hold its breath, too), without haste but without hesitation, Bonhoeffer climbs the scaffold, helps adjust the noose, and dies.

Music may be sprung with the trap door, if a composer knows how to groan for a whole world. The camera moves down the fine body, finding its splendid strength, its readiness for life. The camera holds on the naked feet. Then, a slow dissolve. The feet blur, the streaking gray of the prison wall shifts to tan of sand, and the blue of the early morning sky deepens, brightens to the blue-green of the sea.

As the image clarifies, the same bare feet are in more or less the same position, only now they are lying on a beach. The sounds of youths, racing, wrestling on the sands. A ball may hit one of the still feet, or a young tanned hand grab a foot and suddenly the feet galvanize, stand, run into a full-screen beach alive with surf, sun, horseplay. The sixteen-year-old Bonhoeffer throws himself into the commotion while careful credits are rolled over the carefree action.

---

* The rest of the verse would be ". . . the Lord gave, and the Lord hath taken away; blessed be the name of the Lord."

The Wandering
Years

INTERPRETIVE NOTE I

The ensuing scenes deal almost exclusively
with the complex person and the many-layered for-
mation of Dietrich Bonhoeffer. However they are
arranged, shot, and edited, they must establish in-
delibly Bonhoeffer's full engrossment, participation,
and delight in the whole world. Biographical details, real incidents will provide the narrative struc-

31

ture, but they will be most important at this point in showing us a youth who will be remembered through all the grimmer, later scenes as one whose steady though by no means untroubled joy, from beginning to end, was in living and in the world he lived in.

Certain elements in these scenes will of course be important to later developments in the story. Dietrich Bonhoeffer's brothers and sisters, for instance, must be established swiftly and memorably in their separate and distinct identities. Together they had everything to do with Dietrich's later political activity, and the reference here is not just to the weight of his siblings' later political arguments. In a large close family a brother goes where the others are endangered. There is no understanding of Dietrich Bonhoeffer at all where this simple observation is missed, or where his family is not seen in its vividness, its vitality, its claim on him. Individually, the brothers and sisters figure in the later plotting, imprisonments, executions. Subsequent poignancy will depend upon developing from the first the high individuality of each member of this remarkably close family.

Just as important to later plot developments will be the early theological convictions and the German political premonitions involved in the first film sequences. They cannot be slighted, any more than the family introductions can be.

But the immediate object of the ensuing scenes is to introduce a privileged, brilliant, cultivated, grateful, self-confident Christian man of the world. Casting, obviously, carries heaviest responsibility for establishing all this at once. Appearance, manner matter most. But scenes involving home, travel, the arts, athletics, friends, education, good clothes, and good food, and good drink will help.

Plot lines are just being spun here. They will be threaded later.

STORY I

The beach could be almost anywhere in Europe or America (or even North Africa); the year could be almost any time in Bonhoeffer's early life. For this fine athlete delighted in games, swam often and well, played tennis expertly. And he traveled, thanks to a curiosity that suggested it, intelligence that warranted it, and family affluence that permitted it.

So now, if this scene finds Dietrich in late adolescence, the place might as well be one of the many beaches visited by the Bonhoeffer brothers and sisters in their summer wandering together: one of the Halligen, perhaps. The Halligen are tiny islands which do not even appear in ordinary atlases. As a matter of fact, they barely show in the North Sea off the coast of Germany where

33

they lie. Each sandy acre rises only a few inches above the ocean, with one building (the city hall) crowning the slight rise on each of the islands. At low tide the Halligen are all fine beach; at high tide there is little left of any of the islands but their town houses. Apparently floating, now they are the refuge of the laughing, chattering groups who had earlier been cavorting on the vanished sand. It is the Bonhoeffer group that the camera will invade and introduce.

There will be confusion at first about who is who. Beside whatever other tourists there are on the beach one summer day in 1922, the Bonhoeffers and their friends make a small mob by themselves. Karl Friedrich, the oldest brother, is twenty-three years old this year and already the brilliant physicist who will do crucial work in the development of heavy water, retiring from that research as soon as it becomes clear that it might contribute to aggressive armaments; that episode comes later, but the earnestness and decisiveness of the man should somehow be illuminated now. If he joins his younger companions at all in their game, he drops out shortly to wander away with his fiancée, Greta von Dohnanyi, the daughter of composer Ernst von Dohnanyi.

Klaus Bonhoeffer, who will be in on many of his brother Dietrich's later international adventures, is twenty-one years old this particular summer. Considered the brightest of the boys by his

father, Klaus is already well along in his preparation for the law (he will finally be a chief
attorney for Lufthansa). At some point in the
beach game he might well huddle with his fellow
law students and future brothers-in-law, Rüdiger
Schleicher and Hans von Dohnanyi (Greta's
brother): If Dietrich were to try to join that
group even briefly (say, when the three young
lawyers challenged the rest of the group), he
would be noticed by one of the girls and taunted
as a teen-ager trying to get in with the young
jurists: "You, Dietrich; what do Klaus and
Rüdiger and Hans have to do with you?"
Twenty-two years later Klaus and Rüdiger and
Hans have to die with Dietrich; the Bonhoeffer
tragedy, when it comes, is not a single agony but
a family cataclysm. (When the film comes to that
cataclysm it is not inconceivable that some echo
of some such joyfully derisive cry could filter
again onto the sound track.)

But now the law students are overwhelmed
and separated by the others. Ursula Bonhoeffer,
twenty and the oldest sister, whip-smart and
beautiful, tackles Rüdiger Schleicher, who falls
happily. Later they will marry. Christine, the second sister, nineteen, critically gifted and something of a nonconformist, is even rougher with
Hans von Dohnanyi, who will subsequently be
her husband. Justus Delbrück (Klaus' closest
friend, also a law student) and his sister Emmi
Delbrück (who will later be Klaus' wife) descend
on Klaus. Less boisterous, Dietrich's twin sister,

Sabine—the twins, it will be remembered, are sixteen this summer—winds up on the edge of action with Gerhard Leibholz (of Jewish family—which in this story is not gratuitous information—another law student then, now a justice of the West German Supreme Court). That leaves Suzanne, the thirteen-year-old, beloved baby of the family, shielded from the roughest action by Dietrich, strongest and quickest of the children, and, by his little sisters' testimony, their champion, their knight.

If the Halligen episode is prolonged to end of day, with the whole group driven back by the tide to the city-hall steps, the scene may fade with their singing. Ursula and Dietrich lead in this. A two-part version of a Schubert song would permit distinguishing and identifying the Bonhoeffer brothers and sisters over against the melée of their friends and fiancées, the Bonhoeffers perhaps grouping to carry the harmonic line. One Schubert song, "*Gute Ruh,*" was a favorite of Dietrich's, but it does not lend itself to part-singing. At an early age he had tried to set this "Rest Well" for string trio. The words and the music of the song—in it the stream sings to the dead (quintessential *Lied,* obviously)—might have later thematic utility.

We are meeting here not just a man and his family but their whole milieu. The *Wanderjahre* are convenient to the purpose: the hiking, singing, gallery-going years when the Bonhoeffers and their friends, as so many groups of relatives and friends in Germany at that time, spent long summers wandering over their own country. Short scenes, concurrent or seriatum, will establish the family's cultural context. Conversations begun in one scene may be continued in another, or the sound track full of the talk of these highly verbal youths may be quite independent of the kaleidoscopic screen.

The Heide might flash briefly, for instance: that magnificent, little-known part of Europe, the vast, rolling, sunny, redolent heath of Lünebourg. Christine and Hans von Dohnanyi would be featured in this fleeting scene, maybe even discovering a rocky crevice in the sand. Decades later papers deeply incriminating to the family will be hidden on the Heide; some may still be there.

In the Alte Pinakothek in Munich (a superbly rebuilt museum where period authenticity would now have to be checked, but where some soaring empty galleries and dramatically sweeping staircases beg for a script written around them) Klaus, the eager connoisseur of all the arts, leads the group to the huge Alpine landscapes of their great-grandfather, the army general and painter, Count Stanislaus Kalkreuth. In Hamburg, at the Art Museum, Klaus shows his family and friends the portraits done by Stanislaus' son, their mother's uncle, Count Leopold Kalkreuth.

In Weimar, Ursula would be interested in the

Liszt relics. The Bonhoeffer children's grandmother, Klara von Hase (née Countess Kalkreuth), was a piano student of Franz Liszt and
of Robert Schumann's widow, Klara. The art
school in Weimar had been founded and directed
by old Count Stanislaus Kalkreuth. And the
Goethe sites had special family meaning to the
Bonhoeffers, too.

In Potsdam the younger girls, Sabine and
Suzanne, might be curious about the royal pal-
aces, where their mother's aunt was lady-in-wait-
ing to Crown Princess Victoria, wife of Friedrich
III. The Bonhoeffers' own mother was raised in
the atmosphere of the Potsdam court. Dietrich
would have been more taken with the Garrison
Church in the same capital, where grandfather
Karl Alfred von Hase (son of church historian
Karl August von Hase) was court preacher to
Kaiser Wilhelm II—until he rebuked His Majesty
to his face for having referred to the poor as
"curs." The Kaiser stopped coming, and grandpa
found it convenient to take up teaching at the
University of Breslau.

In Bamberg, Karl Friedrich's agnosticism, always determined but never evangelistic, can enter
the picture. The vast, ancient cathedral with its
two chancels (one at each end of the nave, raised
like the decks of an old galleon) has in the floor
of one of the chancels the worn, plain, mysteri-
ously blank tomb of the only German pope,
buried there a thousand years now. And while
the young scientist wonders to an equally skepti-

cal Klaus about what it all has to do with anything, Dietrich is at the foot of the other chancel
stairs, looking high up on one of the great pillars,
where the famous medieval sculpture of that
"parfit gentil knight" is mounted, he who appeared in every book of boys' stories for generations. (A screenwriter may find thematic suggestion in this familiar knight, or at least symbolic
possibility. The sculpture reappears late in this
Memo. By then childhood's ideas of purity and
valor will have been radically altered for the conspiratorial adult gazing up at it again.)

The older brothers and sisters can make affectionate fun of Dietrich's interest in the sculpture.
The little girls make no secret of the fact that
Dietrich is their knight, and it is not impossible
that he has entertained the image for himself. Ten
years later he is still capable of embarrassingly
romantic self-analysis, meant only for himself,
however. At this point, though, Ursula may recall Dietrich's argumentative distress when at
eight or nine years he discovered that his doctor
father *charged* his patients for his merciful help.
Sabine can recall how she and her twin, while
they shared a bedroom in childhood, would lie
awake imagining what being dead would be like,
and trying to get nearer eternity by shutting out
any other thought of any word but 'eternity.'
Later, when she and Suzi shared a room, Dietrich
arranged to knock on their wall when it was time
for them to "think about God," desisting, at last,
when he discovered that his thumping piety often

woke the girls from their sleep. At war games in their own back yard during World War I, he limited the play to soldier drilling after a sand bomb on the chicken coop terrified a hen off her nest. Which gentle recollection reminds Christine that the worried six-year-old Dietrich had had to be accompanied to school (there was a bridge on the way) though he required that the delegated servant walk on the other side of the street so the other school children wouldn't ridicule the little victim of his own imagination. One of the brothers could even badger Dietrich about his supposed interest in the health of the slender knight and his lean horse: which pill would have been good for which creature. Humorous capital may be made of this throughout the film. As were his brothers and sisters, through his whole life the splendidly robust, athletic, solid Dietrich was worried about everybody's health including his own, and was hooked on pills, powders, elixirs; he was always a traveling pharmacopoea. So the banter will go, letting viewers get to know the family, especially Dietrich.

Other scenes will let viewers get to know Germany, too: the marvelous ancient buildings of Franken; or Swäbish Hall, dear gabled storybook town where Bonhoeffers were buried for hundreds of years; or Cranach, perhaps, with its beautiful Old Town, half-timbered houses on cobbled streets ringing fountained, flowered squares, the great walled monastery beetling down from above exactly as it did centuries ago when Lucas of Cranach was painting there; silvery landscapes from the wintery Wartburg; the Nicolauskirche in Eisenach, and Bach's house there; the little-known cathedrals in Halberstadt and Quedlinburg.

It is all part of the old German culture and art and architecture, and it is all part of the Bonhoeffers. Dietrich and his brothers and sisters did not just live in Germany, they inherited their nation and its splendid treasure. They were the blood heirs of many of the original creators and investors and developers. They defended their country as proud, grateful proprietors. It was theirs to love, to criticize, to defend. Later, for a while, Dietrich Bonhoeffer will interpret the whole crisis of World War II as a fight for the preservation of this Western Christian culture, so nobly exemplified in Germany and then so basely attacked by some low-born, tasteless Germans.

The whole shifting, darting introduction of people and places arrives at last, in the Bonhoeffer home, Wangenheimstrasse 14, in the exclusive Grünewald quarter of Berlin. The house is large and life there is conducted in a manner at once generous and austere. Dr. Karl Bonhoeffer, handsome, reserved, ironic, is professor of neurology and psychiatry at the University of Berlin, of worldwide reputation in his field, unchallengably front-rank in the Germanic academic world. Mrs. Bonhoeffer is the gracious, serene manager of the household and the attentive, eagerly involved mother of the family. Included in the menage are governesses, nursemaids, housemaids, chambermaids, yardmen, and a cook. All of them and everything is unobtrusively, tastefully arranged to make the Bonhoeffer children comfortably, happily at home in a generally hospitable world.

Not that theirs is an untroubled world. A dinnertime scene would permit some show of the family style (two housemaids always served at table); the prevailing religious reticence (after the soup is served the mother asks, "Whose turn is it to pray?" and one of the children then says, "We thank you, Lord, for food and drink, Amen"; no more); and the customary seriousness of conversation (the father permitted nothing obvious, banal, or unimportant from the children). In the summer of 1923, though, Germany is deep in the wild inflation that made life ludicrous and began the electorate's treacherous familiarization with the bizarre. The Bonhoeffers feel the strain, too, of course. But Dr. Bonhoeffer has among his patients his own share of the wealthy American ladies then tracking down psychiatrists all over Central Europe, so the economic trials come through somewhat more smilingly at Wangenheimstrasse 14 than elsewhere. Thus at dessert time Dr. Bonhoeffer could report on what he has done this day with an annuity policy for 100,000 marks (it should have been worth $25,000) that has just matured—a policy on which he had paid dutifully for decades, planning to bank it finally against retirement. The 100,000 marks, it develops, is just enough this year to buy a bottle of wine and a box of strawberries—or so he had thought. Reporting ruefully on his little shopping expedition, he confesses that the wine was beyond him, his policy covered only the box of strawberries by the time he got to the market.

But rue and irony are not the limits to Bonhoeffer levity. Family life though serious is not solemn. That is, superficiality has small place in the household, quiet for study and rest is inviolate, but there is plenty of the joyous commotion of music, conversation, games, parties, too. Everybody plays an instrument (Dietrich is a talented, well-schooled pianist) and/or sings. Evenings that are not given completely to music often end with music. Conversation, when Dr. Bonhoeffer's friends assemble, as they do regularly, is elevated, spirited, and informed, important as the company itself: Adolf von Harnack, Max Plank, Theodor Heuss, etc. In the summer there is much coming and going for tennis and swimming. In the winter, skating fills afternoons and many moonlit evenings; Dietrich and Klaus are especially accomplished figure skaters and dancers. And parties pepper the year. The aristocratic Dr. Bonhoeffer is not beyond disguising himself as the butler and waiting hand and foot on his oblivious—and subsequently dumbfounded—assistants. The brothers and sisters write and perform plays, recite their own odes, make up dances, and as late as his seventeenth year Dietrich is still good for a gold-blond, smooth-muscled Cupid energetically impaling guests on blunt paper arrows. It will help in later scenes if Mrs. Bonhoeffer's high military relatives, the von Hases, can be introduced cordially in these blithe circumstances.

Two important notes about these early sequences: Whatever scenes are contrived to introduce the Bonhoeffer household, it must be remembered that Dietrich Bonhoeffer was himself a minor element in the family. Next to the youngest, he was always one of "the little ones." In the family's regard (including Dietrich's), it was "the big boys" who counted most—the brilliant young professionals, Karl and Klaus; Walter at eighteen the dead hero of World War I. For Dietrich, of course, the same considerations only fueled an already competitive spirit, which was, however, never aimed at outdoing his brothers and sisters but only at deserving their attention and appreciation for excelling in his own field as they did in theirs.

The second important consideration is that the household was never a pious one. The children's early nurture was traditionally religious—that is, it had the usual religious elements—but the atmosphere in the house was briskly intellectual, academic, artistic. Dietrich's decision for theology was understood by his family (his mother's father and grandfather were distinguished professors of theology) but it made no great impression. When the clan got together, the lawyers and the scientists set the conversational stage; Dietrich played his lively part in it of course, but it would have been hard to get the rest of the family going very long on a specifically religious subject. When all were grown, common prayer would have been an embarrassment—probably most of all to Dietrich.

It may be wondered if his mother, though, might not have wished he'd talk theology at home a little more.

The Schooling

The Bonhoeffer family *Wanderjahre* comes to an end about the time that Dietrich begins his university education. Older brothers and sisters marry, start to have their own families, and the mass movements of the clan become impractical. But Dietrich's higher education involves him for several years more—one could say for the rest of his life—in his own *Wanderjahre*. A year at the University of Tübingen is followed by a summer quarter in Rome and North Africa (with Klaus). At the University of Berlin, where he next enrolls, he completes his doctoral degree work and prepares to join the faculty there himself. Before beginning his teaching, however, he has a year's pastoral internship in Barcelona and another year away as Sloane Fellow at Union Theological Seminary in New York City.

The next scenes, therefore, will be in easy continuity with those of the last section. The camera continues to track Bonhoeffer in fascinating places. Only now the travels are beyond Germany, and range farther in time than they did there. The settings go back into Roman and Moorish antiquities and ahead into the skyscraper and slum futurities of America.

But the new action breaks any tendency for the film to go travelogue. For Bonhoeffer is now engaged systematically and full-time in that professional preparation that gives all the rest of the story its special cast. He has decided on a life in the church and is therefore educated as a Christian theologian, Lutheran branch.

The earlier scenes of the family will have been mismanaged if this development is seen as abrupt or forced. The Bonhoeffers, while eschewing piousness, were at home with all the academic disciplines—and in Germany theology is an ancient and lustrous department in the greatest universities. Theologians figured in the family background, and star members of Dr. Bonhoeffer's close circle of friends were scholars whose names will be great names in religious history as long as religious history is read.

Even so, if the earlier scenes are played right, there could be a question about Dietrich's decision for the ministry. It would clearly have been an impossible decision for any of the other brothers —perhaps for any other Bonhoeffer offspring. The agnosticism already noted in Karl Friedrich was not limited to this oldest of the boys. Dr. Bonhoeffer, vigorously anti-Freudian though he was, undoubtedly had his own psychiatric accounting for the religious phenomenon and must have regarded religionists generally with more sophisticated respect than with any very spontaneous admiration. The girls were sharp-minded individualists who in their youth would not have spent more time in any pew than was absolutely necessary (though Suzanne happily assisted Dietrich in his parish work).

Yet Dietrich chose for the church. The profoundest intricacies of personality and motivation are, of course, not available to us so long after the fact. As it happens, they would probably not have been available to our analysis even if Bonhoeffer were still alive: He vigorously resisted such interiorization, such rooting around in the psyche, always. He was as unimpressed as his father was by Freudian penetrations and ventilations.

So we are left noting certain differences in the circumstances of his boyhood which might account for his own subsequent alteration of the family pattern. It is a fact, for instance, that Dietrich and his two little sisters had a different governess than the older children did. Fräulein Maria Horn taught the others; her sister, Fräulein Käthe Horn, taught the three little ones. Both the Horns came from the Herrnhutter Brotherhood, a pious, simple, biblicistic religious group (where Mrs. Bonhoeffer had spent several months of her childhood too), but it is at least possible that newcomer Käthe might have gone about her teaching differently than fixture Maria did. Certainly Dietrich's adoration for his first teacher comes through as qualitatively different than the affectionate comaraderie that the older brothers and sisters had with the supremely matter-of-fact Maria (whose "lights out" command Klaus hexed by putting his preferred reading inside Bible covers—no Herrnhutter could ever crack down on so diligent a student of that black leather volume! Dietrich, though, would actually have been reading the Bible for Käthe, and *before* "lights out").

Furthermore, Mrs. Bonhoeffer herself took over the biblical instruction of the last three children, and again Dietrich's devotion to her must have made something particularly significant of her special relation to his first systematic religious studies.

But most affecting of all must have been the

death of the second son, Walter, in World War I. Dietrich was twelve in 1918. He had watched (as his twin, Sabine, reports) at the station while his mother ran alongside the coach in which Walter was going to the front and heard her calling out to the young soldier, "It's only space that separates us." A few months later Walter was dead, and there were services where the twelve-year-old saw earth as well as space separate the family and where he had to wonder how it was that not just space and earth but God too somehow separated their brother from them. Then the grieving mother collapsed and did not return to her household and its duties for several weeks, living elsewhere in the neighborhood part of that time.

Anyway, at fourteen the twins were together in a confirmation class. Sabine remembers the teaching being rather more moralistic than theological, and she doesn't recall Dietrich talking much about it. But in the course of the classes he began to talk about entering the ministry, himself. He may even have debated the issue with classmate Hans von Haeften, met in this church course, who will later be in the German diplomatic service and a fellow plotter with Dietrich in the resistance. At about the same time that the confirmation classes were going on, General Booth, founder of the Salvation Army, came to Berlin for mass meetings. Dietrich was moved by his personal radiance and excited by Booth's effect on the people—how "carried away" they were, how many were converted. Dietrich, as the youngest there, simply observed. But he wished mightily that he were an adult that night—whether to respond to the General's altar call or not, we do not know, but fourteen is the yeasty right time for such risings.

So Bonhoeffer was set for theology. Nor should it really be a surprise that he varies so widely from his brothers in his vocational choice. As one of "the little ones" he must have felt challenged from the beginning to find a field of his own and to excel on a line of his own. Now theology becomes his own arena. His chosen discipline distinguishes, defines him over against both the sciences and "the careful agnosticism of his father and his brothers" (Eberhard Bethge).

Yet Dietrich Bonhoeffer never wanted to live anywhere but right *in* the family, either. The others were everything to him, so all of his theological writing (with the possible exception of that done at or about Finkenwalde) is a kind of continuing discussion—not debate—with his own beloved lawyers, scientists, psychiatrists. Dietrich was a Bonhoeffer in his own profession, Dietrich was one of the Bonhoeffer men as long as his professional preoccupation was with the twentieth-century facts and had to do with right now . . . hence, his famous "concreteness." His doctoral thesis, for instance, is an extraordinary attempt to combine an exalted theology of the church with matter-of-fact sociological analysis of the church. The virtuosity is plain, but virtuosity was not the point: with Karl Barth *and* both Karl Bonhoeffers reading over his shoulder, Dietrich could do no other.

And now, having mentioned Karl Barth, we come to the last contextual remark necessary for interpreting the next scenes. This has to do with the character of the theological education received by Bonhoeffer in his various schools. It was, in the main, the best education available anywhere and would be hard to shade in the offerings of any era ever in the history of theological education. His teachers were the titans of their time and are still basic referents in universities and seminaries everywhere.

They were, in his first years, mostly the great liberals in theology. Liberal, as used theologically, refers to a brand of scholarship that is now taken quite for granted but that in the years of Bonhoeffer's education still had a fight on its hands. The liberal scholars (who could be very conservative in their politics; some voted for Hitler) insisted that in biblical studies the text of scriptures had to be given the same literary-linguistic analysis that any other ancient text is now given, noting editorial layers, charting changes, picking up discrepancies and variations in early manuscipts. Instead of taking the words of the Bible literally, the liberal scholars took them seriously and insisted that that did the words deeper honor.

In matters of doctrine, liberal scholarship specialized in study of the historical development of ideas, with particular attention to influences and relations to other religions. These students did not mean thus to minimize doctrines; they simply found them truer and more interesting when considered in their total human context than when honored (against every evidence) as flat deliverances from on high.

In theology liberalism trafficked in continuities. God and man shared personality, so they were opposite ends of one grand continuum: Man was or had a spark from the divine fire; men are chips off the Old Block; we are of a piece with God; what is deepest in man is highest in the universe. Thus analysis of our own history and experience and mind can bring us to knowledge of God. Since we are in continuity with God, research in man and his culture will bring men to knowledge of God. Sin is our pro tem failure to live up to the mark, but critical sense and the example of Jesus and our own moral effort will help us catch up. The Kingdom of God is the culmination we are headed for. It will come in history when our best social endeavor builds the Kingdom of justice and peace right here. Continuity is the key: Everything flows into, develops from everything else.

Dietrich Bonhoeffer studied all this with the best teachers the liberal line ever developed. And, as Eberhard Bethge observes, he was "affected by the uncommitted, mild teaching of the great old men of the Berlin faculty." The effect was more in attitudes and standards however, than in conclusions. He was generally fair and open as his first teachers taught him to be. At the end of his life he was contemplating a reconceptualization that would have pleased them by the direction it seemed to be taking. But early in his theological education Bonhoeffer turned down the liberal theology. That happened when, after four semesters at his universities, he read Karl Barth.

One of the hardest problems before you movie makers will be giving credibility to the fact that as recently as forty years ago (maybe even thirty? or twenty?) many contemporaries still took theology so seriously that a Swiss scholar writing in Germany could energize, electrify whole schools of people with his theological reorientation. From 1918 till well up into the 1940s, Karl Barth and Barthianism (also called the dialectical theology and neoorthodoxy) were sensational, even scandalous, in church and academy.

He gave double offense. Against the ever present and always vocal conservatives, Barth bought from liberalism both its literary criticism of the biblical texts, and its historical understanding of dogma. But against the gentle and hopeful liberals, Barth turned down *all* their careful continuities. No; God and man are not located at different places on one continuum of personality: "You cannot say God by saying man in a loud voice." No; God is not to be found by studying man or his conscience or his religious sense or his culture or the natural law or cosmic order: God is *"Totaliter Aliter,"* the Totally Other. No; sin is not a pro tem failure to come up to the patient

God's mark: sin is impatient man's open rebellion against God, "man in revolt," as Emil Brunner called it, ours not the misdemeanor of breaking God's laws, but ours the treason of challenging God's right to make any laws at all. No; our moral effort won't set this straight: God will forgive, but the initiative is completely with him. No; the Kingdom of God is not something we build, but something that God will establish when and how and where he wills, and it will be as apt to condemn as to confirm human efforts.

Karl Barth ripped into liberalism's Sunday nap. The Swiss dealt in abysses and chasms, axing great clefts in all the familiar continuities, and offering Christ as the single bridge. God and men meet in Christ, and in Christ alone. In Christ, and in Christ alone, we see all we are going to see here of God. Christ, and Christ alone, gets us the forgiveness we cannot earn from God. Christ is our only clue to the Kingdom. And for us? We are always in the crisis of decision: every minute yes or no to Christ. And if yes, then the knowledge that Christ was not just decided for, but was in on the deciding.

It all seems to have taken Dietrich Bonhoeffer on a first reading. It is not hard to see why. This teaching must have come closer to his own perceptions than did his other teachers'. Barth helped him to see what he was almost seeing, so he allied himself.

But there were other reasons, too, important to understanding Bonhoeffer's character. Barthianism was, in 1924, a radically new development in theology. It appealed to the young Bonhoeffer, who was by then well into his own field but had not yet developed his own line—and that was important in his family of individualists. Liberalism was current, à la mode, the way a generation already worked; Barthianism was hacking its own way and just getting started. The Bonhoeffer family gave new credit to Dietrich for his identification with a stormy movement just entering the public eye; they now got quite interested in something they were only polite about before.

Furthermore, Barthianism was a loudly verbal development. It was as much style as substance. The way it said what it had to say seemed to establish what it had to say. It was godsend to a preacher, it was pulpit Christianity, it lived on radical judgments and point-blank certainties, it scorned apologetics and made liberalism's modesty look vapid, it fit Bonhoeffer to a T. He was not given, congenitally, to the balanced caution and minimal assured statements of his first teachers.

Besides, Barthianism had a compatible romanticism about it. It peopled reality with great presences and filled space and time with vast transactions. It was also a splendid aesthetic achievement, the work of a titanic genius among those creative artists, the theologians. It is, as all great works of art are, the striking statement of a commanding vision, and Bonhoeffer knew his arts. There was about all this, too, the huge splash of its sudden development. Barth startled the church. His was necessarily a disputatious crowd. Dietrich Bonhoeffer was quite at home in the furor. As a matter of fact, he made some waves of his own. In America in 1931 it was enough for him to speak a straight-line Barthianism: offense was given at once, and the fur was always ready to fly. But in Europe, Bonhoeffer was a critical friend of the Barthian theology with ideas of his own, so the fray was, if possible, even livelier back home.

The schooling to which we turn now didn't all happen in school, but it always featured high talk.

STORY II

The connection with the earlier sequences is without seam. The university years begin in another famous and beautiful old German town, Tübingen, and of course some of the ubiquitous relatives are there too. Sister Christine preceded Dietrich to the university by a semester or two, and together they now live with the splendid old Grandmother Bonhoeffer (who should be introduced here, if only to prepare for a great episode in which she stands out years later).

The panoramic shot, which is the elision between the last scenes and this, sweeps Tübingen, and there it all is again: castle above, quiet, shaded river below, ancient university and town between. Well before the camera settles in on the Neckar River, the sound track fills with the noise —drowsy chatter, sporting shouts, university songs—of students at play. The sport and tradition here is punting—same as on the Thames. The boats are pushed along by poles, braced against the river bed. In some of the little craft, desultory conversations go on, drifting as the boat does. Between others there are clamorous contests. And now and then everybody chimes in on an ancient student song.

Dietrich Bonhoeffer will be in on the fun with a group of his fraternity brothers. The *"Igel"* they are called (hedgehog). A so-called "black" fraternity, it permits no dueling, does not have flag colors of its own. Instead, fraternity brothers wear hedgehog quills in their hats. Throughout the scene, in the soft talk and in the rough-housing, Dietrich is guyed with amused affection by all the others. He is the youngest member of the fraternity (a "fox," as the pledges were called by the upperclassmen, the *Burschen*); probably the youngest for a long time, which makes him the frequent center of attention. There is more affection than amusement in the brothers' references to his distaste for violence of any kind. *Not sure this is your game, Dietrich; somebody might get hurt.* This would infuriate Dietrich—he always played strenuously—but would leave room for joking reference to his penchant for pills, in which amusement outruns the affection: *. . . he hates to see anybody hurt, but he's dying to prescribe for somebody . . .* It was easier to be amused than charmed, too, by the young Bonhoeffer's quick certainties. He was very sure of his own mind, and quite ready to help others make up theirs.

And there was much on young Germans' minds that summer. In the punting repartee someone might use a French word or expression and get the quick freeze. For France was *bête noir* in those seasons. The humiliation and crippling exactions of Versailles were bitterly resented by all the students, who were further inflamed against their old neighbor enemy by France's recent occupation of the German Ruhr. There were riots these years all over Germany. Hitler and Ludendorff had tried their first *Putsch*, disastrously but disturbingly. There was much anxiety about possible invasions from the East.

So, late in the afternoon, as the fraternity brothers straggle up the path to the *Igel* house (behind the castle), talk can get serious. Even in the drinking room to which all gravitate (the "beer church," as a good *Igel* always calls it), there is debate about the appropriateness of in-

terrupting one's schooling for a short training
period with the defense "police" who were being
prepared for duty by a government still denied a
regular army. The Allied Control Commission
frowned on this clandestine paramilitary operation, and was about to clamp down on it, so the
autumn of Bonhoeffer's term at Tübingen gave
the students what looked like a last chance to
serve their country's defense before even this
makeshift was dismantled.

Bonhoeffer is less than overwhelmed by the
prospect of serving so, but reluctant, too, to be
left out. If debate gets rough in the beer church
he can cover his own uncertainty by moving to
the piano where he is the regular accompanist for
the students' singing. Reference might also be
made in the vigorous exchanges envisioned here
to Bonhoeffer's uncanny facility at reading
character from handwriting. He was so clever at
this, as a matter of fact, that his success at it
worried him a great deal. Years later he reported
that he had soon given up his graphological exercise, and never did it again. In scenes set in 1924,
however, it could still be used honestly as narrative ploy.

The upshot of the debate is that Bonhoeffer
does go with his fraternity brothers to spend
some days in a secret military camp near Ulm,
drilling with the so-called "police." The episode
is not a large or important one in his story, but it
does help illustrate the frustrations of the country

which later turns to drastic solutions, and it is of some interest as Bonhoeffer's only close connection with military service.

If legend and letters are accurate, he was a middling "policeman." One story has him offending immediately by throwing his washwater out the window. Sentenced to scrub the whole barracks hall with a toothbrush, he stomps back to the Tübingen classrooms two days after leaving. The spirit of the story is probably truer than its substance, though Dr. Bethge thinks it might have happened to Klaus Bonhoeffer in 1918. It is, however, a good symbol of Dietrich's independence, too. Certainly he did not go back to Tübingen before his two-week stint was up. He even enjoyed the exercises and spent all of his free time with his books. Returning to school he hailed tablecloths, knives and forks, sheeted beds, and warm baths—and worried about the dark truculence of the officers back in the camps, waiting for a remilitarization of the nation.

The actual classes with the Tübingen theological faculty need not be developed at this point in the picture. The general line taken is enough like that to be developed in connection with his subsequent studies at the University of Berlin, so its exposure can be put off till then. If there is any attention given to classes at this juncture, it could be the course with Professor Adolf Schlatter, a biblical theologian who remained very influential with Bonhoeffer afterwards, or a course in Kant with Professor Karl Groos, remembered later in prison, or the course in medieval church history which turned the seventeen-year-old's mind to Rome.

That mind was violently turned off in the winter semester when Dietrich, the acrobatic skater, fell on the frozen Neckar and was unconscious for a long time. His parents came from Berlin, and during his convalescence heard from him that the shock hadn't knocked Rome out of his thinking. The Bonhoeffers—grateful for their son's recovery, celebrating with him his eighteenth birthday, and always predisposed to Rome (it had been the *terminus ad quem* for traveling Bonhoeffers and von Hases for generations)— were at least agreeable to considering the possibility. Dietrich wrote his sisters to talk up the project at home. And by spring, he and Klaus were in Rome.

Again, the panoramic approach to a great city? Dietrich Bonhoeffer was disappointed in his first sight of St. Peter's, but overwhelmed by the Colosseum. He sat pensive in the great amphitheater—even more dramatic then than now, overgrown as it was with vines, palms, cypress— dreaming of an antiquity he could only guess at, peopled here no doubt with the muscled swarming of mighty bodies in deadly collision. The Vatican was, on early visits, most important for his first look there at the naked anguish of Laocoön and his sons and near them the marble perfections of a superb Apollo. The day that he dreamed so long in the Colosseum he ended his diary entry with, "the great Pan is not dead."

It may be wondered whether he couldn't have summarized his whole Roman spring so. Not that he pursued the cloven-hoofed, priapic god while there. Klaus may have heard the merry piping, but then Klaus may have known better how to listen. Dietrich shortly turned most of his attention to the Roman Church and to its cultus. While Klaus investigated classic ruins and modern beauties, Dietrich was going to services. Lent and Holy Week have for long, of course, been high holy days in the church, and these particular celebrations now became high points in Bonhoeffer's religious education. With the guidance of a young Austrian priest, Dietrich went through the whole drama of the Passion in the Roman Church.

If done *cinema verité*, this footage of Easter Week could be stunning: high mass at St. Peter's on Palm Sunday, in a throng of monks, priests, seminarians, of all colors, in all garbs, from all continents; vespers that evening in the Trinitá del Monte at the head of the Spanish Steps (did he notice the Shelley–Keats house-of-the-early-dead at the foot of the Steps?); hours in Santa Maria Maggiore next day watching people, including children, at earnest confession; on Good Friday, five hours in the mob at dark-draped St. Peter's, and back again for radiant Easter. All through, the *sotto voce* explanations of the young priest.

But the prime impressions were far more than intellectual. The music was never forgotten. Years later a radio echo of the Trinitá del Monte vespers will be heard in the Tegel prison cell. It must be so impressive at this first hearing that we too remember in delight and despair when it comes again. The liturgical richness made its own impact: The sounds and rhythms and fragrances of Catholicism's elegant exhuberance unstopped the German Lutheran's liturgical pores. He met a devotion you can bathe in, and though it finally was not for him, it immensely freed his conception of what could be. The sight of confession moved him, too, and again, though he never advised the Catholic mode, he later makes confession an important element in his own understanding of Christian life and community.

But most of all, Rome threw open the windows it is to be hoped were already there to be opened in a smart boy's view of Christianity. Later, Bonhoeffer will be in the front rank of the first generation of contemporary ecumenicism. At that stage he will not think it practical to involve Rome too much in conversations Protestants first have to have with each other. But it was Rome on his first visit which gave him, irradicably, the wide-screen, full-color view of what ecumenicity is—not an accommodation that tight Protestants can somehow arrange among themselves, but a variegated, varicolored very great community which is already there to be gloried in, in a compendious church.

The brothers did do some of their prowling together, though. The Roman episode might wind up with such a trek: Dietrich showing Klaus the admired Laocoön, and in St. Peter's the Michelangelo Pietà, never a favorite of Dietrich's. Later they will gravitate to the sidewalk cafés of the Via Veneto, and in the cool of the early evening watch the other world swirl by. Over coffee they may discuss the Pietà. Gently anticlerical Klaus could comment on the likeness of the pose to the Madonna and Child of tradition—only this one is the mature Christ, still held like a child by the Mother. *That's the church, always babying Jesus.* Dietrich, with no interest in defending the statue, is indignant at the interpretation: *That isn't it at all—he's dead and his mother of course holds him once more, but also shows him, offers him to us. Besides, being childlike isn't bad* (to the end of his life Dietrich was to offer the child as Christian ideal: direct, unreflective, spontaneous). *Jesus himself said "for of such is the Kingdom of Heaven" . . . and I think that text is still permitted by the scholars.* To which Klaus might even more lightly say something about child*like* being all right, but child*ish* is how the church seems to translate it for itself. Here and elsewhere it will be true to Klaus (and to Dr. Bonhoeffer) if they are shown in disappointment not so much at Dietrich's theological interest as at his commitment to as small, peripheral, and weak an institution as the Church.

But then Klaus notices a friend entering a

nearby bar and the older brother prepares to join him. Pointing him out to Dietrich, Klaus explains this is a new Arab acquaintance, member of a noble family (his life long, Klaus counts many friends in the nobility), who has invited them to visit him in Tripoli. Money would be a problem, and the parents' permission would by no means be automatic, so a little quick scheming is necessary before the brothers are in excited agreement on unannounced ways and means—father and mother will be written from Africa. Then the brothers separate, Dietrich to wander and to sit awhile (*holding* his Kant, at least,) in the Pincio, the wonderful park spread around the Villa Borghese at the head of the Via Veneto.

Klaus and Dietrich do steal off to Tripoli, have a wondering ten days in the desert. But the Mohammedan and his culture are opaque and stay mysterious to the brothers. And the visit to the Arab nobleman is a disaster. The brothers never talked about what happened, but they seem to have been more or less dismissed as "unwelcome guests." Friends of Bedouin princes today can well imagine how mistaken the North Africans might have been about young Nordic tolerances in 1924.

Anyway, no lingering in Tripoli. Sicily for a while, then Klaus returns to Berlin. Dietrich is on his own for a few weeks, makes a last visit to favorite landmarks—the Trevi fountain, Pantheon, Spanish Steps—and finds them not nearly so hard to leave as he had feared. It is Catholic

Rome he grieves in parting. A thunderous *Te Deum* in St. Peter's on his last day, and he is off: Siena, Florence, Milan, home.

The education from travel, exposure, cultural osmosis lends itself easily to filming. Classroom schooling, though, is less photogenic. The next phase in Dietrich Bonhoeffer's preparation is at the University of Berlin where he hears lectures, reads books, writes papers, attends seminars. None of this photographs commandingly. A quick shot of Dietrich riding to school on the commuter train as he regularly did with his neighbor and most famous teacher, Professor Adolf von Harnack, would establish Bonhoeffer again in his privilege. The early recognition of his brilliance and promise might also be established if Professor von Harnack—whose eminence would be indicated by the attitude toward him of the other people in the coach—were urging Bonhoeffer, as he frequently did, to follow him in his own field, to succeed him at last as an historian. Even a few words of clarification by Professor von Harnack could reveal the whole orientation of the Berlin faculty: liberal, evolutionary, rational, optimistic, progressive. History was moving onward and upward; religious values in general, Christian values in particular, were being realized; if the nations were off stride at the moment, they would get back; democracy and education were the way.

If the National Socialists were wearing their swastika lapel pins as early as 1924, there might be one on another passenger, vaguely out of focus beyond von Harnack, but providing visual counterpoint to the hopeful remarks.

At parting (careful lifting of firm, expensive hats) the distinguished teacher asks his young student where he will spend the coming term break. At the Bonhoeffer's country home, Fredricksbrunn, comes the answer, batching it with his cousin Hans Cristoph von Hase, a physics student at Göttingen.

Which permits us to pick up the cousins in the next scene, either climbing through the woods to the beloved summer house in the Harz Mountains, or actually in the oil-lamp-lit kitchen, firing up the old cookstove and preparing a meal for themselves. Wherever the two are met, Hans Cristoph has just completely confounded Dietrich. *Not* going on in science, Hans, dropping physics! But that is all you've ever been interested in. What happened? Why?

The answer may begin in some embarrassment, but it goes on to assurance. I've heard another teacher at Göttingen: Karl Barth, a Swiss. In theology. You've got to hear him too, Dietrich, or at least read him. (Maybe an accident at the stove at this point.) See, it's just the way Barth says: All the old answers are like lids that are too small for the pot: Lids that don't quite fit, don't *almost* cover what they are supposed to, they fall right in, they disappear. But Barth's answers are big enough. He got me to reading Dostoevski, for instance, and physicists don't even know how to pronounce him. But the Russian knew: there is a Sodom and a Madonna in each of us. And *we* aren't going to straighten that out, not by education, not by politics. If we're going to come out right, then God has to do it all.

Bonhoeffer, who of course had begun to hear of the controversial new figure in German theology himself, is fascinated, covertly amused, finally deeply impressed by his cousin's experience. He promises to read Barth as soon as he can, though in addition to his regular school work he is now trying to get ready for a Sunday-school class he has agreed to teach back in Berlin.

To which the scene shortly turns, and Bonhoeffer shows soon enough that he has indeed kept his promise, read Barth, and been swept up in this torrential new development. The problem for the film is how now to convey the Barthian style, the violent disjunctions, the radical dependence on the divine initiative, the relative disinterest in all of man's works including his politics. If some idea of the whole is to be attempted in this scene, perhaps there should be a young minister friend of Bonhoeffer's visiting the class too.

Then Bonhoeffer would be discovered in one of his specialties, making biblical points by telling what sounded half saga, half fairy tale: one about a great king, who reigned on a beautiful mountain, and who sent a herald out into the world one day to proclaim some good news, only to have him waylaid, killed by the people who should have been glad for his news, and so forth. Or one about an old woman lost in a snowstorm, coming at last to a closed door that can only be opened from the other side. This was told as an Advent lesson, undoubtedly making the point that the birth of Christ *is* God opening the door from the other side, the only one who can let us in, at Christmas saying welcome. Perhaps this is the story to overhear now, for twenty years later Bonhoeffer is to interpret a Christmas in prison in reminiscent tones: Prisoners understand Advent best of all—always they wait for someone else to open the doors, which can only be unlocked from the other side. If the thematic parallel is attempted later, of course, some sound or image might be repeated from the present scene (but without italics, surely, something subliminal, perhaps?).

Toward the end of class discussion, the talk swings around to current politics. One youth might observe that his father has just joined the National Socialists. Dietrich rejoins lightly, *My father hasn't and won't.* Another student: *Mine won't either, but he does say this "democracy" we've got has to be thrown out and something stronger found.* Dietrich again: *Well, we'll see; maybe not. But really this isn't any of my business. I'm a Christian theologian and our problem*

*here is not how anybody is going to be thrown
out of any historical, earthly door, but Who is
going to let us in the only door that really counts,
the heavenly door, the last door.* That's *what we
have to think about in the church!*

Somehow the lesson ends and the pupils turn to
play under Suzanne Bonhoeffer's direction. She
had been talked into doing this by Dietrich, who
in all his youth work insisted on much play,
sport, outings, fun. This time, though, Dietrich
wanders off to a far end of the room with his
young pastor friend. The latter is admiring,
troubled. *You're a wonder, Bonhoeffer. I wish I
could talk to the little people that way. But then,
I wish I could play tennis your way too, or the
piano . . . Is it enough though? God knows I feel
a traitor even asking that. Barth is my man too. I
was bored to death with all that middle . . . that
middling stuff we were getting. And then Barth
came along—you know, he saved me, made it all
worthwhile. I hate to doubt him now. But is he
really right? Are those last doors really the ones
that worry people? Or aren't all the earlier, intermediate ones—the marriage doors and sex doors
and parent doors and school doors and work
doors and political doors—aren't they the really
hellish ones? The ones we have to go through
every day? And are they opened from the other
side? Or should we be pushing too, the way we
think they ought to go? God, look at our country, Dietrich; who knows what's going to hap-*

pen? But shouldn't Christians be trying to find out, so they can throw their weight where it may count? While there's time? I just don't know . . . I still check first with Barth, I guess, but I'm almost sorry it's so now when I get in the pulpit. The people like the big sound—Barth likes Mozart but he orchestrates like Berlioz—but they know it's too easy, and now I'm beginning to know it's too easy. Our man isn't clear enough about what matters right now.

Bonhoeffer's answer would be flat. *Who knows what matters now? Only God sees that. You preach His Word and that is everything. Just preach, and let the chips fall where they may.*

The young preacher desists: *Maybe you'll never have to know what I mean. You're planning to join the faculty some day, I suppose—the professors are certainly expecting you to—and the students will take whatever you give them, for a while yet, anyway. But don't forget me in my little parish, where the people either don't take what I give them, or take it and make nothing of it, or take it and make what they want out of it.*

Dietrich is eager to get into the games, building up in the background. *I'm not so sure about that faculty post. As a matter of fact, I'm thinking more and more about a little parish too. Just a simple little job as a simple little assistant in a simple little German church in Barcelona!*

And on the word Barcelona the screen and sound track erupt into Spanish scenes, color rhythms, sun. If the last sequences have been long on talk, the pictures can move again now for a while, flashing from all the different parts of the screen. Bonhoeffer, in his year in Spain, visited Majorca, Madrid, Toledo, Córdoba, Seville, Granada, Algeciras. Sometimes the visiting Klaus was with him, sometimes he was alone. Together the brothers even hazarded another royal Arab party in Tangiers—Klaus had a knack with invitations—and this time all went well: milder Caliph? or older, wiser brothers? Everywhere it was the people who took center stage for Dietrich, the proud, independent, vivid people, radical egalitarians across the most rigid cast lines and economic distinctions anywhere. Cathedrals claimed Bonhoeffer (has Barcelona's extraordinary Gaudi ever been featured in a movie?) as did museums, especially with their wrenched, luminous El Grecos.

If the travelogue is going rapt, let it explode again now in the bullring. Nonviolent Dietrich, taken first to the arena on Easter Sunday afternoon by Klaus, a bedazzled *aficionado* himself, turned into a bullfight fan, and even had a fling at it himself. It was for him a ceremony, a ritual, the aristocratic expression of an old culture, and so more a part of his aesthetic affirmations than his moral inhibitions.

So was the Picasso! He and Klaus found the cubist oil in a Madrid market. The canvas was

74

signed "Picasso" and the style was right. Efforts to substantiate the claim were never completed, though. Picasso himself would not comment, except to observe that a Madrid friend could paint a lot like him. Museums were interested in the brothers' find, and prices offered went from 5,000 Reichsmark to $5,000—which were not offered for phony Picassos in 1928. The picture hung in Klaus's Berlin home for years, always the object of attention and the subject of good-natured debate. It was destroyed in the fire-bombing of Berlin in 1945, as was Dietrich's favorite Spanish acquisition—a copper brazier that became a fixture later in the Finkenwald seminary, and for which he longed in icy prison cells before his death.

And then there was his church in the German colony of Barcelona. This debut in the pastorate seems to have been sensational. He joined German clubs where he played tennis, sang in a chorus, played the piano, attended parties including a masked ball, played chess. He impressed with his good clothes (it should be remembered throughout that Dietrich Bonhoeffer always dressed well, ate well, drank well; he was an incessant theater-, concert- and opera-goer, and his tickets were always well placed). His preaching was so preferred that the senior pastor stopped announcing ahead of time who would be in the pulpit on Sunday. Bonhoeffer attempted counseling sessions, and ran into exactly what every other young minister in a great city does:

the panhandler. There is a classic complaint from Bonhoeffer: The counselee doesn't give you the whole story, you take a chance and give him something, shortly you discover you were taken in, you get sharp with the next applicant—and deeply wound an honest, innocent man. Bonhoeffer had his usual Sunday School class, of course: one girl, the first week; fifteen boys and girls, the second; thirty, the third; and it never went below that again.

During all of this, the ideas continue to grow. He is more and more confirmed in his swing to the massive Reformation doctrines reclaimed by Barth. Principles, values, ideals are the enemy, and action oriented to or by them is anathema. Tolstoy comes under the interdiction, because his pacifism was obedience to a principle instead of faithful waiting for a specific ethical command from the God known only in Jesus Christ— which word might be pacifistic and then again might not *but don't try to guess it ahead of God's command*. The same strictures rule out all conscientious objectors. Anyone who makes a law or principle or ideal of anything, no matter how high-sounding, must be exposed as an idolator, a usurper, one who puts a value in the place of God —whose specific command for specific occasion can only be waited for.

So Bonhoeffer remains obdurately out of the political argument that followed Germans to Barcelona. Statecraft was still none of his business as a theologian. He was, furthermore, a vocally proud and grateful child of Germany and a champion of his misunderstood nation.

Only two new motifs enter in Barcelona. One is Don Quixote, read there in Spanish, and brooded over for a long time, later to play his part both in theological and political comment. The other is Gandhi. The remarkable Grandmother Bonhoeffer gives Dietrich money for a trip to India, thinking that it was time for him to get next to the other great world religions too (the psychiatrist's mother!). Dietrich, making modest noises now about peace, would go especially to meet Gandhi if he could. The trip does not come off this time. But the interest grows, the money is reserved for this use alone, and plans will be revived over and over again.

The return to Berlin may, perhaps, be omitted in the screen play. If so, certain details from the year and a half Bonhoeffer now spends at home will have to be noted otherwise in later scenes. The swiftly escalating political turmoil, for instance, will get close attention shortly. The fact is that on his return Bonhoeffer becomes acutely aware of a new temper in Germany and a new tenseness, apprehension in his own very liberal family. He, however, continues to hold himself aloof from the political simmer, giving much of his time instead to the writing of his second, highly technical theological book, which will give him access to a teaching post at the University of

Berlin. The only development in his own thinking of any direct relation to politics is the steady growth of his interest in pacifism. The almost-trip to India and Gandhi continued to work its suggestion.

Then, in June, 1929, Bonhoeffer spoke at the state funeral of his great teacher, von Harnack, hailing him as "the champion of the free expression of a truth once recognized, who formed his free judgment afresh time and time again and went on to express it clearly despite the fear-ridden restraint of the majority." In July, Bonhoeffer delivered his own inaugural address as the remarkably young *privatdozent* at the University of Berlin. But before he began his teaching he was to have one last year of postdoctoral education, this time as Sloane Fellow at the Union Theological Seminary in New York City. Even as he left he was looking forward to his return and reunion with a new friend, the closest friend he had had till now, Franz Hildebrandt, a young Protestant theological student, whose father was professor of art history at the University of Berlin—and whose mother was Jewish. With all his brothers and sisters married now, Dietrich's friends became more and more important to him and to his story.

And then, New York. This is another juncture where the screen will be most faithful if it manages to swarm as Bonhoeffer's busy mind did with impressions, novelties, expansions, jolting surprises.

There are dormitory scenes and there are classroom scenes. In Hastings Hall, where he lived, the young German was in smiling despair over his American confreres' incessant cheeriness (making an encounter of every passing in the halls) and their blithe disregard of privacy, barging in wherever and whenever they wanted. He was to change his mind some on both: the students' familial regard for each other figured in his own later thoughts about Christian community, and according to at least one other student Bonhoeffer himself became pretty good at barging in and staying for long talks.

In the classroom he was most interested in the history and analysis of American thought, philosophic and sociological. He was less interested in what passed for American theology, taking the floor himself repeatedly to sponsor a 100 proof Barthianism, still raising shocked incredulity in American students.

Most interesting of all would be a closer look than we have of his reactions to the discussion of pacifism going on at Union those years. Students, in whose theological thought principles and values and ideals still figured high, were apt to be pacifists. Reinhold Niebuhr, vivid and vigorous new professor of social ethics, was a sharp and telling critic of such principle. While not a Barthian, he was a renewer of great Reformation doctrine, especially the doctrine of original sin, and so, in an invariably if not inevitably flawed world, sought more discriminate judgments in the use of power than pacifists generally allowed. Professor Niebuhr's appreciation of Gandhi, for instance, was not for his noble adherence to the principle of nonviolence, but for his politically canny arrival at a power strategy (nonviolence) which took full advantage of British Christian reticences (Anglican engineers won't run over Indians prone on the track).

Dietrich Bonhoeffer's personal perplexities will be paralleled in the public debate. Knowledgeable and sophisticated as any theologian about the dynamics of society and the role of power, suspicious as always of principles of any kind, he could not simply espouse the current pacifism. But nonviolent by nature, tenderly concerned for the people and things threatened by violence, worried about European developments that portended war, and more and more attentive to the peace command of the Sermon on the Mount, Dietrich Bonhoeffer increasingly leans toward a position congenial to pacifists.

The classroom scenes will be useful in introducing Bonhoeffer's particular friends at Union: Jean Lasserre, a French pacifist who will back Bonhoeffer on that point; Erwin Sutz, Swiss, and Paul Lehmann, American, both lean, intense theological sophisticates who will reinforce Bonhoeffer's intellectual defenses; and Frank Fisher, handsome young Negro student from Harlem.

It is with Frank Fisher that Bonhoeffer gets to know uptown New York. Much attracted to Fisher personally, and disaffected by what he sees of the tepid white church, Bonhoeffer shortly spends most of his church time in the Harlem church, attending the moving services, glorying in their music, teaching Sunday-school classes, leading youth groups. With Frank, too, he visits Philadelphia, then Howard University in Washington, D.C., sees in the capital the symbols of our justice and freedom, and is refused seating in a fine restaurant because Frank is with him (Bonhoeffer's exit is noisily haughty, furiously indignant).

There are other expeditions: repeated trips to travel offices and docks with Paul Lehmann, looking for passage to India for the reactivated visit with Gandhi (Bonhoeffer was dining certain evenings of each week in a greasy spoon, to add to his savings); to record stores with Frank Fisher, buying the spiritual records that will be heard often in later European scenes; to the tennis courts, but not with Paul Lehmann: "It is not fair to those who play well if those who don't take up the time and space," said Bonhoeffer, but smiling; to many concerts, plays, operas, Toscanini at the Academy of Music in Philadelphia, Bach's B-Minor Mass in Carnegie Hall (Sutz sang in the chorus); a Christmas trip to Cuba with Sutz.

Then, toward the end of this first American visit, Bonhoeffer drives a borrowed, beat-up

Oldsmobile to Mexico. The trip almost didn't come off. Dietrich repeatedly flunked his test for a driver's license—he thought—because he wouldn't cross the examiner's palm with a bill, but Paul Lehmann reports that they were in Chicago before competence really dared peer out of tremulous hiding. The car itself doesn't help much either. Its owners urge the young men not to return it: just drive it till it dies. Erwin Sutz, who tries to drive it for a mile or two somewhere in Pennsylvania, is so traumatized by the independence of front wheels from steering wheel that he never again tries to drive any car. Lehmann leaves the party in Chicago, Sutz drops off in St. Louis, and Lasserre sticks with Bonhoeffer to the Mexican border, where the car collapses, and thence to Mexico City on the train. On their return they have some trouble re-entering the country; only wires from Paul Lehmann and from the German Embassy finally permitted them to cross the border and to reclaim the renewed Olds. Bonhoeffer leaves for Germany very soon after his return to New York.

If time permits, there might be some point in summarizing Bonhoeffer in these last days of his systematic schooling (which is certainly not the end of his education; *that* comes April 9, 1945). The occasion would be the Mexican trip. While Lehmann is along, the Europeans could tear into the American deficiencies: the monstrous injustice of white Christians to black compatriots (in

1931 Bonhoeffer saw this as *the* crime that American Protestantism might never recover from); the lack of language training for preachers, the shallow theologizing, the ignorance of history, the disinterest in confessional standards (creeds), the sharp division between church and state, the storytelling preachers and their innocuous sermonettes, the awful choirs with their breathy vibratos on trashy anthems, the operatic soloists, meat-loaf suppers, Ladies' Aids. And Lehmann couldn't agree more. Alone between Chicago and St. Louis, the three Europeans may admit to themselves, though, that these funny American churches do have an extraordinary vitality, people may go for the wrong reason but they do go, credal sloppiness seems to have engendered ecumenical warmth, the churches so separate from the state have a good deal more to say and do about politics than in most other setups (Bonhoeffer especially thoughtful about this), maybe there's something to be said even for homiletical brevity and clarity, new as that idea might be. Alone with Lasserre, Bonhoeffer would turn again to the question of pacifism and nonviolence. Cannot, should not the affection and intellectual community of this young German and this young Frenchman (which has so impressed their American fellows) suggest something more for Christian hope and international possibility? However handled, the main point is that Bonhoeffer by the time he leaves New York has the peace command at the middle of his attention—and recollection of socially active churches tucked back in his mind.

On the way back to Germany there is one important port of call, one last university lecture added to his schooling. By arrangement with Erwin Sutz, Bonhoeffer visits Bonn and sits in on a seminar of Karl Barth, his long admired but never met teacher, who had left Göttingen for Münster and then for Bonn a few years earlier. From first encounter, the forty-five-year-old Swiss professor and the twenty-five-year-old German *Privatdozent* hit it off well. At the seminar table, Karl Barth introduces a subject, asks a question. Discussion and debate ensue around the circle, and Bonhoeffer speaks his first words, contesting or clinching somebody else's point by quoting Luther: "The curses of the godless sometimes ring better in the ears of God than the hallelujahs of the pious!" Barth is delighted (it is exactly the kind of quote for this juicily human theologian of the big books), asks "Who offered that?" and takes Bonhoeffer with him when the class is over.

The three weeks in Bonn are a delight for Bonhoeffer. He is dazzled by the theological virtuosity of the master teacher—and encouraged to find his own voice, developing its own line (not always harmonizing but usually interesting) in the chorus of disciples (poor Barth: he always claimed that he did not want to develop Barthians, that he was not one himself—yet was always surrounded by prickly thickets of them and, as Bonhoeffer would discover, did not really like it much when a student had ideas that went far beyond Barthian ones). The whole state of Bonhoeffer's thinking as his schooling ends and he begins his work in Germany might be summarized in an evening colloquium in Barth's own home. Even after three weeks, Bonhoeffer is not fully received by the full-time Barth students ("It is hard for my kind of Negro to pass for white, here," he reported later, "they check on my fingernails and my foot-soles."). When the evening group is gathered, there is long silence in the Presence, broken only by much pipe business, every student smoking exactly Barth's pipe.

Then someone mentions the Günther Dehn case. This gives the film a chance to edge into the political storms that have been generating during Bonhoeffer's absence abroad. For Pastor Dehn's appointment to the faculty of the University of Halle is being widely protested. And this, because of his earlier stout defense of Ernst Barlach's great expressionist bronze protesting militarism and war, placed in the Magdeburg Cathedral while Dehn was dean there. Even among Barth's students a few may give some idea of the red-hot nationalism now burning through the citizenry and the affront it has been to many in the nation for Dehn to retain the monument. But for Barth it is the perfect social ethical issue for a Christian.

85

His own scorn for all political conservatives is clear, but he regards that as the private political judgment of one resident. As a churchman his opposition to political unrighteousness will be limited to those places and instances where the political power invades the church or competes with the church *on the church's own ground*. Here is such a case. The church, which is clearly out of bounds if it tries to be a force in political life, has every right to defend its own boundaries, order its own life, define its own beliefs. So Günther Dehn is entirely right if he turns down the parties or even the government (as he did) when they would make partisan political gestures in the church. But the same church does not then join those parties' or that government's active opponents.

The doctrine is familiar to the student. It was to be maintained, actually, long into the Nazi era in Germany. As a demonic government strangled humanity ever more systematically, and tormented ministers asked in growing desperation what they ought to do, Barth would still be counseling that they go on about their preaching "as if nothing were happening." He meant, of course, to rebuke those who claimed the Nazis were seeing to it that *everything* necessary would happen and to encourage those intimidated by the turmoil. But his phrase was at least equally susceptible to the quietistic interpretations which it promptly got. And Bonhoeffer in July 1931 is already impatient with such ambiguous teaching.

He has just come from Jean Lasserre with his drive for international peace *now*. He has just come from Harlem and Frank Fisher and the terrible social inequities that should not be asked to wait. He has just come from an American seminary where slum ministries were themselves generating the political pressures necessary for remedial action. So, though he agrees with Karl Barth that ethics must develop naturally out of faith, that the Christian watches and waits for God's specific commands, Bonhoeffer hopes that the watching and waiting will lead shortly to *seeing* so the church can speak out, maybe even take a lead on at least a few things that are clearly in the political domain too: peace, say, and social justice. Karl Barth, admiring his young friend's spirit, appreciating his ends, finds him impetuous. Dietrich Bonhoeffer, revering the theologian, worries about how cautious he is, how marred his keen awareness of events is by a curious insensitivity to their tempo.

Just a few days back in Germany, and Bonhoeffer is already aware that whatever is happening is not waiting. Both hate and haste are in the air.

The Spoilers

The movie's political stinger is in the next sequences. These will cover the years that should have been Bonhoeffer's good years but that went very bad very soon. Now he was to begin his teaching at the university, something of a celebrity from the start because of his youth. He would be living at home, besides having a place of his own, near again to the whole beloved family. He would be preaching to university students on Sundays and working with slum area teenagers during the week. He would build a summer house for his young charges, and help set up what would today be called a coffee house in a workers' quarter. He would be traveling widely again in Europe in connection with the ecumenical movement of which he was an early leader.

It was all his kind of life. Add sports, the theater, the opera, family musical evenings, and you have the recipe for very good years. If they went bad, it was just because of where and when they were. In 1930 Bonhoeffer left a homeland where it was obvious that something was going to have to give: Unemployment mounted as the economy collapsed further, morals and morale went down together. The Communists and the Nazis (the latter *very* small in 1930) offered themselves as extreme solutions; middle parties were more familiar but peculiarly lethargic. In 1931 Bonhoeffer returned to a country where the Nazis were the largest single party in the national parliament. This was no surprise, of course. He could read newspapers, he had had his family's regular reports. But until he stood again in Germany he could not have realized the extent to which things had gone.

And here is where the political stinger comes in. For how to represent the way things were? It would be impossible to chronicle the whole troubled history, and that is not our point in this

film anyway. This is not one more anti-Nazi
movie. It is a movie about Dietrich Bonhoeffer
and if it is faithful to him and what he was about
then it is a film about us, too. And where more
transparently than here?

For now in swift, separated scenes with overlapping action and dialogue, a twentieth-century
people can be shown struggling with the apparently standard twentieth-century issues. Everything will depend upon writing and playing these
scenes straight, honestly, about Germany in the
early 1930s. Everything will also depend upon
playing them without one single verbal reference
to Germany or Germans or Nazis or Hitler or
Europe. Let there be not one ranter before a
monstrous rally, not one goose-steeping soldier.
The actors will be in homes, schools, churches;
they will be earnestly, nervously debating law
and order, race, inflation, international monetary
crisis, war, anticommunism, internationalism,
keeping the church out of politics, long-haired
youth, respect for the flag, urban immorality,
censorship. *For those were the issues current
then.* Fascism was then as it is now one response
to those issues. This is a case where clarity depends entirely on ambiguity. And ambiguity is
insured if the dialogue accompanying these community scenes refers always and only to "our
country," "this government," "the people," "the
old parties," "that new party," "those people,"
"this nation."

These smashingly generalized scenes become

specifically German again when the nation turns to the politician who has played most notably on its fears and promised a renewal spiced with retributions. Then the basically earthy loyalties that always shaped all his thought and action are shown again in Dietrich Bonhoeffer. There are few in his generation who have as clean a record as his *vis-à-vis* the Nazis. Many of their victims, many notable resisters went along for awhile in the beginning. In their nation's condition they felt that almost any firm hand had to be given a chance. But there is no evidence that the Bonhoeffers were ever taken in for a minute. In Dietrich there was no high, carefully-thought-out principle involved in his almost instinctive reaction. It was aristocratic horror at this vulgarization of his Germany; it was contempt for the trash that presumed now to be responsible for a superb cultural inheritance. Then, as the scabrous outlines of the new regime became clearer, there was added to Dietrich's disgust his anxiety for beloved people. Again, though he was to write and act impressively in the field of human rights, it was no noble principle that moved him first in this field, but visceral terror for an esteemed brother-in-law and a dear friend, both vulnerable Jews under Hitler's incredible law. Concreteness is not where Bonhoeffer comes out in his theology; it is where he goes in.

Anyway, the screen play will pick up Dietrich Bonhoeffer again now as he turns to his own work within the German church and university.

He is as full of "the earth and its creatures" (his phrase), as joyfully absorbed in the world's offerings and its issues as ever. With the acceleration of German political developments antipathetic to what he loves, and with a great personal distaste for violence, he is more and more interested in calling and working for peace. Yet the theology otherwise most congenial to him does not encourage flat declarations of a social ideal for "the earth and its creatures" nor direct involvement of the church in such contingent matters as politics. It holds instead that the only appropriate way for the church to defend the world is to defend the church's own integrity. By defending ultimates, penultimates will be served, and the church is the place to defend ultimates. Bonhoeffer does his best in the next years to organize his resistance within those limitations.

Adolf Hitler saved the reputation of such Barth-style ethics by making theological claims for the Nazi ideology, and by reaching to reorder the church's life to his own taste. His invasion of the church made Barthian and Barthian-style resistance look like a stormy political action by the church. It was not. It was defensive, rear guard action, and not one that would finally satisfy Bonhoeffer. He always knew what his great teacher only tardily realized: that the church should not have to wait to identify and resist murder until it is murder in the cathedral.

But in these early years, he worked mainly for the church's purity.

The political discussion at the end of the scene in Karl Barth's seminar leads directly into short, overlapping scenes, summarizing the political issues before the nation and suggesting the dynamics back of the Fascist take-over.

One such scene might project a troubled bourgeois couple, serious, nervous, not at all "bad" or "wrong," talking about law and order in terms of unnecessary violence, and respect for the police, and safety in the streets. That scene could bleed into another, dialogue switched in midsentence and finished in another voice where respectable men in a restaurant or beer hall discuss the same issue in terms of rowdies and aimless youth with their long hair, their folk songs, their wandering. In neither discussion will causes be a matter of interest nor will justice be important enough to mention. Just control.

In a third scene pleasant, responsible-looking businessmen in an office will be discussing with all dignity the problems raised by "the other race," especially the agitators among them, who are of course Communists. This dialogue can shift in midstream to tea-table women just as upset at what Communist agitators are doing to "those people" (though everybody has a good friend among them, some even a relative). As heads get closer together and whispers generate horror and glee it will appear that there are very personal differences too which account for the ambiguities of attitude that come out as racial censure. Even a wisp of ". . . back where they came from" may be heard.

In a fifth scene gentle old folk will be honestly agonized by inflationary threats to their security, hoping for almost any strong government that can save their small substance and so their painfully calculated future. On one of Berlin's raunchier streets at night other old people, just as nice but not quite as gentle, will react as might be expected to the high school prostitutes and transvestites cruising the clubs where lipsticked, corseted Junkers paw them fatly.

In still another scene a father may yell at his son that "not every forty-year-old is a criminal and an idiot for the simple reason that he is twenty years older than you are" (a certifiable quote; as Richard Freedman remarks about it, "at least the cut-off date then was forty"). The son would not be guilty of a *non sequitur* if his response brought up the fact that in the recent past right-wing extremists had got away with 354 murders while twenty-two left-wing assassins had been severely punished.

Military men may be pictured assuring already

assured military men that big military forces are essential to peace, that civilian governors know nothing of military matters, that peace depends on big preparation and overwhelming strength, that there are worse things than war. Farmers in the field will mouth the same line and add to it contempt for "internationalists," for worrying about what other countries think. The same line can shift to a parish scene where ministers inveigh against "ecumenism" and the idea that other continents, other denominations have anything to add to their own superior tradition. And still another scene where church laymen agree vociferously that politics should be kept out of the pulpit and that the economy is none of the church's business.

Meanwhile, concurrently with these community scenes, on the screen, the Bonhoeffer story might be developed in its own scenes.

One of the first of these would show an elderly professor introducing the youthful lecturer to a surprised but respectful class. The traditional German university applause—the rumble of shoes shuffled and stomped on the hollow wooden amphitheater floors. A young woman student may be one of the gentlest stompers, but also one of the closest listeners.

Another sequence might have Bonhoeffer in full pastoral regalia, preaching to the student congregation at the technical college where he is concurrently chaplain. The girl noticed in the lecture-room scene may reappear in the congregation, may even leave the church with the young minister.

For with Dietrich Bonhoeffer, as with all diarists, there are shadowy figures who are obviously important to the whole story but who never get spelled out in the middle of the page. (Initials often suffice to remind the writer: initials—the detached alphabet of unnoted episode, rendezvous, adventure. A whole new world literature could probably be spelled with those charged, forlorn letters, all those pulsing, abbreviated incognitos, the initials of the diarists.) In Bonhoeffer's case none of these wraiths is more important than a girl whose name (at her own request) does not appear in the biographical material so far available but who began about this time to be an important part of his life. It will be appropriate for her to make her first appearance in these sequences, a silent but active element in the story. She should be written into other later scenes too, even when not noted so in this memo. We will call her Hannah.

In another scene Bonhoeffer will be on his way to one or another of the ecumenical conferences that will keep him on the move throughout Europe for the next few years. In the two years being covered at the moment (1931–1933) this early and youthful ecumenical leader attended meetings in England, Germany, Switzerland, Czechoslovakia, and Bulgaria. In all of them, everyone wants most to know what is happening and what is going to happen in Germany. And in all of them Bonhoeffer pleads for peace, for common action by the separate churches, influencing their governments toward decisions that might conduce to peace. At Sofia he even tries to re-activate his old plan to visit India and Gandhi.

Some of the most interesting of these Bon-hoeffer scenes will involve him with the confirmation class of teenagers he now adds to his other responsibilities. Working-class toughs, these youths have already bullied an earlier teacher into giving up (he died shortly after), and are now ready to take on the fastidious dandy who conde-scends to them from heights of Grünewald and university. Only he does not condescend, and *he* takes *them*. Garbage rains down on him as he climbs the stairs to his first meeting with them, but he doesn't miss a beat. They test him, and he waits them out. (Literally: One roughneck opens a sandwich and starts eating it in the middle of a class period; Bonhoeffer stops talking, watches in total silence until the accelerating, ever more shamed gulping is over; lecture resumed, mid-sentence.) He outswims them, outplays them. His stories come from his own travels. He moves into the poor parish, and his room is always open to the boys. He visits their families and upgrades still further his earlier hesitant regard for the Ameri-cans' slum ministries. He buys one boy a bicycle; he sits with another boy seriously ill in the hos-pital, though his care makes him late for his uni-versity lecture; he buys bolts of cloth and chops off a suit-length apiece for their confirmation clothes; he tries out a new catechism that he thinks they will understand better than the standard one; he takes ten of his charges to his family's summer home for two weeks, most of them away from Berlin for the first time in their lives, and only one window is broken in Friedrichsbrunn

During this confirmation class sequence, the Bonhoeffer scenes may begin to relate directly to the concurrent or intercut community scenes. On some outing or other, the boys may be amused by a gentle, early intimation of political collisions in the nation: the well-documented contest between village bands—one liberal, one radical right—trying to outblow each other on the square.

Shortly thereafter intensity is built by cutting to a political rally, with the Bonhoeffer brothers restless before the tepid liberal lecturer. Klaus, turning to Dietrich, says that's not what it takes. When student screamers howl down the speaker, Karl Friedrick says that's not either.

Suddenly, in a new scene, the screen is full of police clubbing young demonstrators in a summer twilight on a great city's streets. On the sound track, Adolf Hitler's 1932 rasping that the streets of our country are in turmoil. The universities are filled with students rebelling and rioting. Communists are seeking to destroy our country. Russia is threatening us with her might and the republic is in danger. Yes, danger from within and without. *We need law and order.*

Once again the goal in the contextual community scenes (including these last ones) is complete calendar ambiguity. Thirty-five intervening years have to go curiously accordion-pleated and translucent. We must wonder whether it is then or now up on the screen. But the scenes must be edited for acceleration too. Starting easy, the whole sequence whirls at last to full screen-size headlines (January 30, 1933) announcing Hitler's accession to power, which in turn dissolves into a full screen close up of Dietrich Bonhoeffer, never tenser, never more forceful, speaking into a big standing microphone in what then shows itself as a main studio in the German radio. It is February 1, 1933, the day after Hitler's take-over. Without altering a word, Bonhoeffer is delivering the address he had planned to give when invited before the new regime was established. He pleads powerfully against the whole leadership principle as it changes from the proper leadership of a father, a teacher, a governor to the personality cult of one politician. Such leaders can only become misleaders, he insists. Do not go that way. . . . Quick cut to the control room, where the government producer chops one hand into the other ordering that son-of-a-bitch off the air. Dignified bewilderment down in front of the microphone, while a security agent in the control booth makes a note of the incident and the name, and we know a file is now begun on "Bonhoeffer, D."

A telephone call to the studio, relayed by Franz Hildebrandt (who will be with Bonhoeffer in most of the scenes covering the next few years), will ask for Bonhoeffer's radio manuscript for inclusion in an early issue of a scholarly journal, and will invite him, too, to repeat his speech in March at the world-famed German College for Politics.

The dissolve to that academic setting will find Bonhoeffer at the end of the disputed lecture: "The fearful danger of the present time is that above the cry for some strong authority, some powerful office, some firm leader, we forget that each man, each of us, already stands alone before the ultimate authority, and that anyone, *anyone*, who here lays violent hands on any man is breaking eternal laws and taking upon himself a super-human authority that will finally crush him. The fact that each individual belongs to God, smashes anyone who runs against it. A leader rightly leads by virtue of his office, but both the leader and his post must point beyond themselves to the ultimate (final) authority. Leaders or governmental agencies which set themselves up as gods mock God and the individual who stands alone before him, and so such leaders and agencies must perish. Only a leader who can do his penultimate job and in so doing serve the ultimate authority— only he can be called faithful."

After the lecture a little knot of churchmen will detain Bonhoeffer in discussion of his speech and the whole situation developing rapidly in church and state. This enormously complicated history will not be traced in the movie, so its essentials should be compressed into the discussion that follows. Neither will the bewildering roster of actors in the church-state drama be duplicated for the movie. They were far too many—and far too few would have any pride in being reminded now how they acted then. Among those identified at this point, even if mostly for future reference, Martin Niemöller should be one and Wilhelm Niesel another.

But there are others, too, and at first their talk will be full of the astonished or worried reports of what is going on in the nation: the stacking of government offices with Nazis, the pressures on the courts, the lifting of habeas corpus, the censorship put on journals and the capitulation of editors, the first concentration camps, the threats against Jews, the purging of university faculties. "In our time a culture is known by its exiles." Let the list emerge here of those gone or whispered to be on their way: Thomas Mann, Albert Einstein, Paul Tillich, Bruno Walter, Bertolt Brecht, Walter Gropius, George Grosz, Otto Piper— Marlene Dietrich.

The burning of the Reichstag is brought up, too (end of February, 1933), and Bonhoeffer may be queried by Niemöller whether he knows how the psychiatric examination of the accused arsonist, van der Lubbe, is coming. Political liberals naturally hope that Dr. Karl Bonhoeffer, chief of the medical inquiry, will discover something that proves van der Lubbe acted for the

Nazis who wanted a dramatic occasion for their new laws. The Nazis want van der Lubbe identified as a leftist radical, thus justifying their own terrorist rigors. But Bonhoeffer, somewhat stiffly, responds only that his father will make a strictly medical analysis, with *no* political overtones.

Then the talk turns to the church in all this. One optimist reminds the group of a phenomenon now taking place in churches all over the country; whole companies of brown-shirted storm troopers are marching into church services, swelling generally sparse congregations. It is clear how pleased and excited a couple of the preachers are by this. But Niesel (who since these years has been known as "Iron Wilhelm") will have none of it: They are there to cow the congregations and nothing else. But the hopeful churchmen are not cowed by Niesel: No matter why the troopers are there, it is our great chance to evangelize this whole party, we must take advantage of the chance God himself may be giving us. Either Niesel or Bonhoeffer would tick off the compromisers: Of course the self-servers will be satisfied, all those people listening, and such warming statistics; of course the pietest will be grateful, politics being none of his business, and meanwhile all these new souls to be prayed over; of course the theologian will relax, the government is obviously religious, and now he can quietly go about his bookish task.

But—and here was the strength of the Barthian line that held Niemöller, Niesel, and Bonhoeffer together—how did all this fit with the church's understanding of itself? Whenever, wherever it comes to the state telling the church what it had to believe, or how it had to organize its own life, then there must be resistance. We do not like much that is going on in the state, but we are loyal citizens; we fight only if it crosses over into the church. The people now called "German Christians" (pro-Nazi Church members) must be battled by every means open in the church. Their heroic Nordic Jesus must be stopped in his tracks, their revelations through a new prophet, Adolf Hitler, must be scorned, their sacraments of blood and soil must be blasted. If the government insists on a new office in the church, the "national bishop," who can pull the churches together, then from now until the election every effort must be made to elect Friedrich von Bodelschwing instead of one of the "German Christians."

The limitations in this bold line will be shown up, though, if Bonhoeffer's twin sister, Sabine Leibholz—arriving obviously troubled and late in the discussion to sit with Hannah and Franz—draws Dietrich aside as soon as the session is over to tell him that the family has just had private word that the government will shortly dismiss all Jews from public office (her own husband will be exempted from this order by direct action of President von Hindenberg who lifts it from all World War I veterans of Jewish descent; but at

this time, March, 1933, Sabine Bonhoeffer Leibholz does not know that).

Dietrich Bonhoeffer hurries after Martin Niemöller to give him the news. Niemöller is shaken,
as Bonhoeffer is, but contains himself better. It
is clear at once to both that since university teachers are state servants in Germany this will immediately expedite the purges there. Bonhoeffer
points out that in a state church this might even
make a problem for pastors considered Jewish by
Nazi standards. Niemöller hopes not. *But if it
does?* presses Bonhoeffer. *Then we would have
to discuss that,* agrees Niemöller. Discuss *that?*
Bonhoeffer is unbelieving. Discuss *that—when
this monstrous thing, which is a crime wherever
it is imposed, and should be condemned everywhere in the name of common humanity, when
it comes into the church you would still only*
discuss *it?* The older man is deliberate this time:
*It would be a question of strategy, in the hypo-
thetical case of which you speak, Dietrich; we have
very important matters of theological purity to
defend in the church. We will need support on
these too. We cannot this early dissipate our
strength, so needed for central matters, on more
peripheral concerns.* Bonhoeffer is as angry as we
shall see him in this movie: *Peripheral concerns!
Theological purity! Well, if it is theology we should
die for, what is this issue but theology? The
Christian church let us in on the day that St. Paul
triumphed over the Jerusalem party, the group*

that said men had to be circumcised before they could be Christians; now this government tells us in effect that men cannot be Christians unless they and their fathers and their grandfathers are uncircumcised. The Nazis are the Jerusalem Christians this time, but it is the same issue: something you have to do, some way you have to be before you can be Christian, some fence around the church. St. Paul hit that, we have to hit that, it is as central as any issue ever will be.

Bonhoeffer's intensity is terrible. Niemöller knows it cannot be handled by argument. He quotes a revered authority: *Karl Barth and I have already spoken of the possibility we are discussing. He agrees that with so few pastors actually affected by any such ruling—what would it be, ten, twelve in our province?—we should wait for a more central issue.*

Bonhoeffer subsides, but in deep disappointment. Niemöller ends the discussion with appeals to Bonhoeffer and the two young women to concentrate now on von Bodelschwing's campaign. *The church must be kept free. We must beat every "German Christian" candidate.*

Dietrich and Hannah put Sabine and Franz between them and the little group heads for home. *So it will be the church. Not the Jews. The church . . .*

They do jump into the campaign, though. Dietrich speaks to students, especially at the uni-

versity. A line from a Reformation Day sermon
he had preached six months before—von Hindenberg was in the congregation—could be developed
here if he is heard speaking (he would not be the
first or last preacher who referred to old notes;
they all do it: —the best repeat themselves, the
worst quote themselves). *So, we keep saying with
our Luther, "Here stand I, I can do no other."
Everything wrong we do in the church, everything wrong that is forced on us, we get used to,
and then we make it noble by saying "Here stand
I, I can do no other." With such a formula we
think we can make crime Lutheran! We laid the
Old Reformer away, and now with such non-
sense we keep him spinning in his grave. Of
course we do not have to stand here. Of
course we can do other. We do not have to take
what is being pressed on us. We can turn down
the party. We can still vote for a free church and
then take that stand!*

For some, this quote or its equivalent will be
the prime clue to Bonhoeffer's historic significance and sufficient reason for this movie. One
German, one German family *could* do other, and
did. They paid, they died, but they did "do
other." So it was possible; against every piteous
crawl-out, it was possible.

Other quick scenes show Dietrich and Franz,
Dietrich and Hannah, duplicating brochures, dis-
tributing handbills, tacking or chalking up post-
ers. On one such excursion they will be attracted
by a crowd collected in front of a Jewish store,

prominently labeled as such and with storm troopers picketing the doors. This is one of the high points in the chronicles of the Family Bonhoeffer. For there, to the grandchildren's terror and delight, is the ninety-one-year-old Grandmother Bonhoeffer, stepping out of a cab to part the crowd with a look, coldly staring down the picketing bullies, sweeping across the sidewalk and into the store where she has always traded.

Paul Lehmann and his wife visit Bonhoeffer late this spring (April, 1933) and hear the parents calling the Leibholzes daily in Göettingen, to get news or to give news. Evenings with the family seem as pleasant and musical as ever. Only Klaus rises regularly during the evening, even in the midst of innocuous conversations, to walk quietly to one door or another, and then just as quietly but very suddenly, open it a crack. And the sonatas and quartets do not always get the old undivided attention. Some subdued conversations seem best carried on under the music. It could be that in one such evening word is received from Hildebrandt that von Bodelschwing has won. And in another, a month later, the news that von Bodelschwing, whose few weeks in office had seen him unmercifully harrassed by the infuriated Nazis, has resigned. Then, in quick succession, new elections in July, with Bonhoeffer going down to the Gestapo prison (where Dietrich will later spend some of his last months) to protest the seizure of church headquarters office equipment by the police (who now have another entry for their Bonhoeffer file), and with Hitler himself making an election eve pitch for the "German Christians" (he spoke between the acts of a festival performance at Beyreuth), who then get 70 per cent of the vote; the immediate appointment of a Nazi "national bishop"; the so-called "Brown Synod" of September where church delegates wearing the Nazis' brown shirts accepted for the church the state's Aryan legislation.

Dietrich Bonhoeffer is bitterly disappointed— and perhaps even more bitter than disappointed. For he could not have been much surprised. He and Franz Hildebrandt immediately try to get the loyal ministers of the church—of whom there were thousands—to strike. It was an entirely novel idea, which got exactly nowhere: It roused only consternation ("not to bury anyone as long as the government's man was in church office?") and contempt ("How long did you say young Pastor Bonhoeffer was in America?")

Now that the anti-Jewish legislation was visited upon the church there was some slow resistance growing to that. But it was late, as usual, and therefore defensive, as usual, and finally self-serving as all action is which is delayed until a general offense hits you.

And even when von Bodelschwing assembles a theological commission in Bethel to write a declaration that will make clear the grounds for a church's resistance to a state presuming to make its own church, the reception of the mild document (so mild, Bonhoeffer won't sign it) adds to the disappointment. Many, apparently most Christians are loath to say or do anything that will jeopardize the remaining privileges of the church. They rebuke Bonhoeffer and his friends for a rigidity and stubbornness that will spoil all these new chances to reach and evangelize the masses. Why quarrel about theological issues that do not matter a whit to all these new people in the pews? If a few small compromises will get peace and quiet in the church, for heaven's sake why not?

One risky sequel to the Bethel exercise came when Hitler's Reichsbischof, the crony Müller, called Bonhoeffer in to account for his criticism of the government's new church order, a criticism he had based on the Augustana Confession. Bonhoeffer begins his response by quoting the whole section in Latin—until cut off by the bumpkin bishop, far beyond his depth, who says in a weak fluster they will talk about all that another time!

By fall, Bonhoeffer and Hildebrandt are wondering about their place in such a church. Bonhoeffer has heard from two German congregations in London (directly, and through the officers of the German State Church) who would like to have him sent to the English capital as their pastor. Disappointed in what seemed to him homeland equivocations, indecisive about his own next step at home, ready as ever for travel, and hopeful that Franz could go with him, Dietrich wants to accept.

So the two young men present themselves to young Dr. Heckel, external affairs officer for the national church, who must approve, appoint, and dispatch. The encounter could resonate with the major significances of the movie. It is, indeed, one option for the beginning of the movie. If used as a main thread, it could even bear the full weight of the film's plot.

For Dr. Heckel is not much older than Bonhoeffer and Hildebrandt; he is at least as personable, intelligent, well schooled as they. He is cultivated, contemporary, sophisticated—and ambitious. So he sits on authority's side of the desk and the other two sit where visitors sit.

Heckel is not a bad man. In ensuing scenes he will appear again and again as over against Bonhoeffer. The collisions are real and sometimes sharp. But they will lose their depth and poignancy if Heckel is made a simpleton or a criminal. He is a theologically informed, patriotic servant of God and the church and himself—in that order. His ambition was for God and the church in a time that seemed to give them their main chance. He went along.

Which was exactly what damned Heckel for Bonhoeffer. Personally, there was an appeal, a certain mutuality, deep calling unto deep. The young churchmen appreciated each other's brains and ability. They talked the same language, loved some of the same things, laughed at the same time. And that could mean only that Heckel *had* to see all that was involved in the German scene —and he chose wrong. *Chose* wrong; he was not deceived, not uninformed, not stupid. He chose wrong, and so he was the respected enemy, resisted but not hated, doubly damned in a hell of tragic ambiguities.

Later in the *Memo* he will appear as Bishop Heckel. He makes it.

At his last appearance he will be foreswearing both the regime and his office in horror at what Hitlerian Germany comes to. And then he disappears.

But at the time we meet Dr. Heckel, he is the state church's affable external affairs minister, being waited upon by Bonhoeffer and Hildebrandt. He is not at all averse to the idea of Bonhoeffer's going to London. In fact, having had earlier recourse to the relevant file, he thinks it might not be bad at all for him and his colleagues to have Bonhoeffer at least that far away for a while. And, honestly admiring Bonhoeffer's abilities, he knows it will do the London congregations good. And, all urbanity, for Bonhoeffer himself, London is, after all, London!

As for Hildebrandt, why not? That file has been looked at too, and this is a man who is better advised than he may yet know to get away. Though of course there is no hint of that on the face or in the voice of official blandness. Heckel doesn't like Aryan paragraphs either, but he stomachs them.

Things sharpen only at the end of the interview. It is clearly understood that any criticism of the German government on their part while in England will mean immediate recall. The scene can close, then, with Bonhoeffer's vigorous assurance that he never has and never will say anything injurious to *Germany*.

Interlude

The London interlude was a little idyll between storms. It is not entirely clear what Bonhoeffer thought he was getting into by going to London; mostly he was getting away from the slapping he had had to take from a part of the world he adored and from a church he had honored. Theologically he could assign penultimates their secondary place. Personally they were always close enough to the top so he could not bear their betrayal.

But as it turned out, the most clairvoyant tactician could not have devised a smarter strategy than Bonhoeffer seems to have stumbled into. For by being in London when he was, he was able to detach from the Nazi church an important, sensitively located group of German congregations. And by being there he was able to interpret the church resistance as it developed in Germany, claiming for it the ecumenical attention and affirmation it would never have had if he had not been where he was at the time he was (the German state churchmen would otherwise have prevailed internationally with their view of the resisting church as a sorehead, spoil-sport splinter deserving no serious attention).

Above all, though, it is in the personal connections he made with highly placed people that the chief importance of these next nineteen months resides. Important Englishmen get to know, admire, trust Dietrich Bonhoeffer, and that has much to do with what he is finally able to do on the world's stage—and with what finally happens to him.

STORY IV

The London scenes are on the screen what they were in fact—a sudden release from the tension of the last months, a breather before the dangerous years ahead. So, from the taut tensions of the last scene in Heckel's office, the dissolve takes the two young ministers from where they sit together before his desk to where they now sit together playing four-hand Schubert at Bonhoeffer's Beckstein in the living room of the Forest Hills manse. It is a large house, but cold, so most of the living is done in this room before the fireplace.

There is talk: about the two parishes Bonhoeffer and Hildebrandt serve, Sydenham and St. Paul; about the mice on which they mount their hopeless war; about their housekeeper who has suddenly gone mad (religious madness, Bonhoeffer reports), leaving them to cope; about keeping all the Germans in London informed about what was really going on in Germany; about Bonhoeffer's incessant telephoning to his Berlin family, and the British telephone company's giving him a reduced rate because he gave them such massive custom; about London winters, English heat, and about Bonhoeffer's pills and potions; about Barth's testy letter ordering him back to Berlin; about developments in the church at home.

As Bonhoeffer relays word of the development of a Pastor's Emergency League, and describes it as the first nucleus of the organized Resistance in the German church, the scene might dissolve to the study of George Bell, the gentle, sophisticated, sympathetic little Bishop of Chichester (who will be very big in the rest of the story), to whom Bonhoeffer continues the report. By spring of 1934, resisting pastors assembled at Barmen declared the new government of the state church heretical, and set up an emergency church government, the administrative units of which would be called the Brethren Councils of the Confessing Church. The resistance church is now known as the Confessing Church. And the point Bonhoeffer is hammering away on to the Bishop is that since the state church is clearly apostate, the Confessing Church is not a second German denomination but is *the* church of Germany. Bonhoeffer's audacity is as imperturbable as his aim is steady. He knows exactly to whom he is speaking. Chichester is a presiding officer in the principal ecumenical organizations of the day (he would later be a president of that World Council of Churches in which they all issued). By inviting the state church to international meetings as *the*

German church, he can scuttle the Confessing Church. By inviting both churches, he can give a wrong connotation altogether to the development of the Confessing Church. But by inviting the Confessing Church alone, as Bonhoeffer urges, he will declare before the world what the real situation is in Germany—and he will, at the same time, enlarge the churchly status of the ecumenical organization, which will thus be seen as an organ of discriminate Christian judgment and not just an administrative front for adamantly separate churches. Chichester was never able to accomplish all that Bonhoeffer urged, but he agreed with the young man, moved the ecumenical bodies to go much farther on Bonhoeffer's line than they otherwise ever would—and the two men loved each other dearly.

Bonhoeffer pushes the same argument everywhere he can find listeners in London: to the other German pastors; to the other German congregations, to youth groups meeting in his house, choirs practicing there, Christmas pageant players rehearsing there; to the Dohnanyis and the Dresses when they visit; to Berlin students Wolf-Dieter Zimmermann and Jürgen Winterhager when they come to stay a while. He gets Chichester to help find jobs for the refugees piling in from Germany; he cleverly parallels Goebbel's annual Winter Aid Collection in London with a special collection for the relief of Jewish refugees now in England. It is all very much part of the church struggle in Germany, but it is exuberant, almost blithe, away from the governmental threat.

Then Bonhoeffer's success brings the German government back in. It becomes clear that under Bonhoeffer's pressing the German congregations in London will take themselves out of obedience to the state church and align themselves with the Confessing Church. Heckel flies over. At a reception given the smiling, reassuring bishop he gives a radiant picture of the revitalized fatherland, and explains away all of Bonhoeffer's "misrepresentations." Parishioners are persuaded, and take Bonhoeffer aside to rebuke him. Bonhoeffer makes strong rebuttal, to Heckel's discomfiture, but to the waverers' satisfaction. At parting, Heckel cannot resist observing that at his own request he will be received by the Archbishop of Canterbury two days later. It is a setup for Bonhoeffer: at *Canterbury's* request he will be going to Lambeth *tomorrow*.

Cut to Bonhoeffer's cab driving through the tower gate of the ancient redstone palace on the Thames and down the immensely long courtyard to the archbishop's residential wing. The Bishop of Chichester meets him at the door and escorts him to the primate's study. There is a long, cordial visit, with Bonhoeffer reporting on the arrest of ministers in Germany. He is assured by the Archbishop that his warnings will go directly to the highest levels of the English government, and that the Bishop of Chichester will be empowered to write President von Hindenberg with the strongest possible protests against what is going on in the German Church.

At parting, Chichester may ask the Archbishop whether he will be needed the next day at the meeting with Heckel. Canterbury does not recognize the name at first, then dismisses it briefly. *Won't receive the man here at all. It was his idea, anyway, not mine. I'll give him fifteen minutes at tea somewhere in the City.* But then the Archbishop walks Bonhoeffer through the broad halls with their portraits of predecessors (Wolsey, in cardinal crimson, high on the Great Hall wall), and down the grand stairs to his car, urging him to come again soon, come often.

News from Germany insures that the London interlude is just that—a breathing space between engagements. Useful as Bonhoeffer is in England, he cannot stay away indefinitely. The Roehm massacre in July 1934 scuttles any last hope that given time, reason will prevail in Germany, that once obstreperous critics will be able to return to quieter participation in a rational state.

Accusing his henchmen, Ernst Roehm of personal depravities as well as treasonous ambitions, Hitler looses his forces on all his known enemies. Horror is piled upon horror. On "the night of the long knives" murder and summary execution is the way. No semblance of legality is contrived. Brute power and violence over-ride all the traditional forms of justice. A servile Ministry of Justice announces that everything done was necessary and right.

Now the face of the monster is in full sight. Bonhoeffer had suspected that this was what Germany and the world were up against, but he had hoped he was wrong, that maybe argument and persuasion could affect the new overlords. *That* hope is pole-axed by the overlords in this mid-summer nightmare. The opposition is not reasoned with, it is wiped out. Bonhoeffer hardly knows what to make of the fact that not a minister is killed: respect for the cloth? contempt for the ineffective? or just no real resistors in the parsonage? Gratification wrestles with humiliation. Humiliation wins when old friends in the Confessing Church join the national chorus hymning Hitler for the Roehm purge (a pervert, ugh) and saving Christendom from Bolshevism.

So vision clears. Bonhoeffer and some others see what they have to do with—and whom they have to do without. President von Hindenburg dies in the same summer, and Adolf Hitler becomes Der Führer. Opposition cannot stay at a distance; it must move now toward hand to hand.

The last scene is back in the manse parlor. Hildebrandt has been in Germany, helping with the Confessing Church. Bonhoeffer is full of the London Germans' break with the German church, and of his own participation in the ecumenical conference on the Danish island of Fanö. There he had fought hard for the strongest possible declarations against any kind of war at all and for the rights of conscientious objectors. He remembers being asked one afternoon at the beach what he would do if he were conscripted, and then hearing himself say as he watched the sand slip through his fingers, I would pray for the strength not to bear arms. In this connection, there can be rueful comment on his latest aborted visit to India. This time he had a personal invitation from Gandhi to come, he had lined up his shots, he had the money, but then it all came to nothing again. And just when he wanted to find out all he could about passive resistance.

Viscerally despising the Nazi state, Bonhoeffer was shopping for effective resistance tactics—and since, in resistance to a militaristic tyrant, any kind of pacifism runs directly counter to The Leaders' expansionist ambitions, Bonhoeffer was increasingly given to pacifist speeches both in Germany and on his ecumenical trips outside Germany. Whatever his technical theological reservations, pacifism was at this point a tactically useful political weapon. But beyond that cool appraisal, there was also his equally visceral delight in the good things of the world and the gentilities of a great culture; his deepest human orientation turned him naturally toward gentleness and sensitivity and the cherishing of life, so his exhortations for peace were native, too. And then there were the happily remembered months at Union with pacifist Jean Laserre, and reunions since, regularly reinforcing the affection and respect for a serene friend's strict reading of the Sermon on the Mount.

For all these reasons, Bonhoeffer's abhorrence of war and violence and killing could not be scripted too energetically here. The more memorably they are put now, the more forceful the drama, shortly.

For the main talk is about the bid to Bonhoeffer from the Confessing Church to return as director of one of the remote seminaries it has had to set up to train its own ministry. Bonhoeffer has been visiting Anglican monasteries and retreat houses to get some idea of what Protestant separated group living and learning might be. Now Hildebrandt and he are to go to the coastal area northeast of Berlin to find a suitable place for the school. They are excited. But London has been lovely.

Maybe the fire flickers low, maybe the Schubert "Rest Well" is chorded slowly, softly on the piano, maybe Hildebrandt muses: So the nonviolent head back to violence. And Bonhoeffer: The free are going to lock themselves in again. Hildebrandt: The ecumenical return to keep a church split. Bonhoeffer (striking a more vigorous chord?): And I can hardly wait to go. Hildebrandt: Or to come back.

The Tunnel

These will be tricky years to act and to photograph. For some sweet folk, with a winsomely "spiritual" definition of religion, these are the most attractive Bonhoeffer years. This is the time (1935–1937) when he takes himself off to quiet retreat, to the supposedly untempting rural reaches, to contemplation and Biblical meditation

and much, much prayer. Even better, free
prayer. These are the years when he is putting
together earlier experience and ideas which even-
tuate in two inspirational books, *The Cost of
Discipleship* and *Life Together*, Lenten classics
from the moment of their English translation.
This is the time when Bonhoeffer the churchman
tends strictly to the church's business—before he
goes off the rails and gets all mucked up in political filth.

Yet for other Bonhoeffer devotees these are
the embarrassing years, the years they want to
explain away, the years their own hero has un-
comfortable second thoughts about later, though
he did his best to put a good face on his confusion.
These are the years some would subordinate as a
"detour," Bonhoeffer off his own main road. Such
true believers are offended a little by what they
think is a break in what they would like to see as a
slow but steady confluence of gospel and world in
Bonhoeffer's thought. They are put off by what
looks like some kind of monasticism. They would
rather skip this retrograde movement back into
concern for the *church's* own purity and welfare.

Bonhoeffer himself would probably understand neither his admiring nor his disgruntled ad-
mirers. For him, these were just the next years.
Though he carried them off with his usual flair,
they were not easy for him. There is some evidence of an otherwise undocumentable personal
crisis, a private turmoil which Dr. Bethge insists
should not be called a "conversion"—there is

hardly a more un-Bonhoefferian word (if un-Bonhoefferian is a word). But the disclaimer is interesting. At any rate, whatever happened, there is a sharp interiorizing observable about now. His devotions became more strenuous, his Biblical exegesis and preaching more subjective, improvisational, he was not afraid of the charge of monasticism.

Still, in the interpretation being essayed in this memo, the years in the *ad hoc* seminary will not be called a retreat, nor should they be filmed as such. They are instead, granting Bonhoeffer's development so far and the developments in his immediate environment, a logical next step. Some walls are closing in, all right, but he is still going ahead. These years are a tunnel, going his way, with light at the end where the walls will fall clean away.

What had happened was that those prime Penultimates, the state and its church, went sick at the same time. No wonder Bonhoeffer felt confirmed in his renewed allegiance to the abiding, unchanging Ultimate, and no wonder he felt justified now in a temporary and partial disengagement from the disappointing Penultimates. Yet the disengagement was never really that. Bonhoeffer was never half as worried about what impious men could do to Ultimates (what *could* they do?) as he was worried about the vulgar havoc they were wreaking in his dearest Penultimates. Nation, politics, church, institutions, manners had gone bad. "In that moment," reports Dr. Bethge, "Bonhoeffer turned to the ultimate for the sake of the penultimate itself."

So hindsight shows us now. At the time, though, Bonhoeffer would probably have had trouble explicitly ordering his priorities so. Yet the years in question are littered with evidences of his discomfort in his declared theological position and the priorities and limitations it assigned. Everywhere in those years, the world and the worldly assert the independent weight and significance they *always* had in his life.

As a matter of fact, all the interiorizing mentioned before might just as well be termed aggressive exteriorizing. That so-called monasticism, for instance, was not at all what the word sometimes suggests. It was a very cool phenomenon. No hothouse luxuriating in its own warmth, this was an outfit for the preparation of a cadre, a troupe of braced, ready men. The meditating and the exegesis and the writing had everything to do with the recruiting and training and equipment of a cadre that stayed on stand-by alert during its training. Bonhoeffer's continuing participation in ecumenical activities had become important to him almost completely for the help other churches might be to his church in its struggle. Even the phrase with which Bonhoeffer stirs a scandal at this time, "he who severs himself from the Confessing Church, severs himself from salvation," theologically indefensible though it may be, is strategically superb.

And if it be objected that all this aggressive

activity is still only for the church and its health, there are other signs that show what it is and who it is beyond the church that make the church's health important.

Peace is what it is all about, and not just peace in the church. Peace in the world is a main burden of *The Cost of Discipleship*, a book built of the seminary lectures. Life, freedom, justice for the Jews, and not just baptized Jews, is never more clamant with Bonhoeffer than in just these years: "Only those who cry for the Jews are allowed to sing Gregorian chants!" He and Hildebrandt beg their church to be "the voice of the dumb." His theology may have been under strain, but Bonhoeffer now as always acted to save who and what were important to him in ways appropriate and available to him at the time.

STORY V

If the last words in the London episode were accompanied by a crashing chord on the Beckstein, the chord itself is accompanied by a crashing surf on the cold, bright, bare beach in the Baltic dunes of Pomerania that now fill the screen. Fighting the winds, running, gasping, laughing, Bonhoeffer and Hildebrandt have just caught sight of the half-timbered, thatch-roofed resort house which will be the seminary's first home.

This is Zingst, April 26, 1935. Since the seminary has permission to use the shore house only until the swimming season begins (June), there is no use going into much detail about it. Bonhoeffer and Hildebrandt will find Wilhelm Niesel waiting for them, though, and with him a few of the new seminary's first students (Niesel, superintendent of the whole theological education effort of the Confessing Church, has brought the young men out from his Berlin office). Other youths straggle in across the barren, chilly sands. Pastor Wilhelm Rott, two years younger than Bonhoeffer, will be his assistant. Student Werner Koch, who will later be involved in very dramatic incident, should be identified.

And then, soon after Niesel and Hildebrandt leave for Berlin (Franz is assistant to Niemöller there in a Confessing Church parish), the tall young Saxon, Eberhard Bethge, arrives—enters the seminary, enters Dietrich Bonhoeffer's life, enters this story. After Bonhoeffer himself, this is the role that will take most careful casting. For though the whole personality may be illuminated in the next few scenes, the first impression on the audience must be what it was on Bonhoeffer that blustery day, what it still is on those who meet Eberhard Bethge: the splendid size and strength of the man, the open face and the glad, free laugh, the fine mind, the beautiful voice, the gentle spirit. From here to the end (except in New York and in the prisons—and there too, sometimes) Bethge will be with Bonhoeffer. Bethge will get the important letters from the prison and later give them to the rest of us. Bethge will inherit most of what Bonhoeffer had to leave as an estate. Bethge will become Bonhoeffer's literary executor and biographer, marry his niece (Renata Schleicher), father his grandnephew (Dietrich Bethge) and grandnieces (Sabine and Gabriel).

In our day of bargain-basement psychiatry it will take a special effort to establish cinematically the strength and wholesomeness of this friendship. For its pattern, one must go back into the manners of German romanticism, rather than forward into the supposedly better informed but far tenser tentativities of today. It would be impossible to overstress either its natural beauty or its importance to Bonhoeffer. Damon and Pythias. Jonathan and David. If Dietrich and Eberhard do not join them it is only because the German names overfill a classic mouth.

Anyway, if Zingst is shown at all, a quick dissolve should discover the same beach five or six weeks later, now warm and glittering, with the twenty-five students out for a last swim, a long evening of talking and singing in the hollow of a dune (the thin purity of four-part Josquin des

Prés; Bethge is already stretching and sophisticat-
ing Bonhoeffer's previous musical tastes).

Then, the invasion and conversion of an abandoned boys' school in Finkenwalde, same general
part of the country, but inland a bit. Here the
seminary will stay to the end. The architecture is
undistinguished, and the gymnasium is badly
built, but there are many rooms and the gym is
turned into a chapel. The students do the carpen-
try and the furnishing. Two Becksteins dominate
the main room. Rembrandt prints are changed
regularly on the walls. Bonhoeffer's big record
collection is moved in as are his books. Music begins to fill the old building: Negro Spirituals
from the record player, with young Germans
trying hard for the rhythm, and Bonhoeffer ex-
plaining; on one piano or two, more familiar
strains of Chopin, Brahms, even the *Rosenkava-
lier* waltzes; choral groups working away at
Schütz, Schein, and Scheidt (oh marvelous row!).
Enthusiasm over the daily schedule, once the
community settles down, is not unrestrained.
Bonhoeffer's classes are notably successful—
which is as well, since he teaches almost everything. But some of his ideas for community life
meet real resistance. Daily chapel is compassable,
especially with Bonhoeffer leading in vernacular,
matter-of-fact, free prayer. But the half-hour of
meditation, just looking at and thinking about a

Bible verse without any scholarly or practical agenda, is revolting. And there are revolts. After one of Bonhoeffer's trips to England on ecumenical business (he was a globe-trotter to the end) he returns to find that his assistant has let the students give up the meditation. That evening Bonhoeffer explains that the community is of course a democracy *except on the issue of meditation*. There, he cannot remember asking for either advice or consent. Meditation is reinstituted.

He is less successful with "lunch" and the reading during lunch. Bonhoeffer's preferred English-American light meal at midday is immediately a scandal, a Teutonic treason. That lasts one day. The reader, droning through elevating literature for the speechless munchers, as the monks did in their great, chill commons, lasts hardly longer.

Another classic Christian element reclaimed by Bonhoeffer justifies itself shortly among the preliminarily abashed youths. A kind of "confession" is instituted, more spontaneous than formal, but perservered in. At first a general confession of irritations and antagonisms clears the air, when the seminarians speak to each other frankly but privately and individually about what bothers them in each other. Thereafter, the always personally reticent Bonhoeffer suggests that each choose one colleague who will from then on hear one's confession and remind one of our forgive-

ness. So Eberhard Bethge becomes Dietrich Bonhoeffer's confessor and the infinitely absorbtive
young Saxon stands steady while his distinguished
young dean confesses, deplores, asks to have
broken the pride that spoils every accomplish-
ment. And that will finally see him through.

The men are to help with the housekeeping, of
course, but their alacrity is not always up to their
principal's standard. When they are laggard about
clearing the table, one day, Bonhoeffer does it
himself and then locks the kitchen doors while he
washes the dishes himself, giving remorse no
chance to work itself out. Another day he finds
an unmade bed in the dormitory and makes it
himself, sheets pulled as tight as his lips. Not all
of Bonhoeffer's ideas for the community hold,
and there is some give even in those that do, but
there is a daily discipline.

And it is for a purpose. Bonhoeffer knows
there is a fight up ahead. He is vigilant for any
signs of a wrong idea of what the seminary is all
about. So, after a long, full day of study, sport,
settling in, in a drowsy evening bull-session, one
student may say something about how good it is
to be separated a little from all *that* (waving his
arm toward Berlin, the outside world). Another
student may parody some of *that*: Hitler ful-
minating about Communists and disorder. Still
another can mimic a stout bishop, all pious hope
on law and order and the government's obligation
to use force. General agreement that Finkenwalde is better. One even quotes Psalm 133:1,

"Behold how good and pleasant it is for brethren to dwell together in unity."

Bonhoeffer's entry on all this is a little sharp. Just do not get carried away, do not get *too* far off. The rest of his speech could be a colloquial version of these sentences in his *Life Together* (p. 1): "Jesus Christ lived in the midst of his enemies . . . So the Christian too belongs not in the seclusion of a cloistered life but in the thick of foes. There is his commission, his work." And once Bonhoeffer gets wound up, he could go on with a quote from Luther: "The Kingdom is to be in the midst of your enemies. And he who will not suffer this does not want to be of the Kingdom of Christ; he wants to be among friends, to sit among roses and lilies, not with the bad people but the devout people. O you blasphemers and betrayers of Christ! If Christ had done what you are doing who would ever have been spared?"

Bonhoeffer goes to Berlin weekly to teach his university class. There he gets late news from his family and from Niemöller and Hildebrandt and carries it back to Finkenwalde. The men who wait up often seat their teacher on the steps before he can climb to his room and there hear and discuss his reports.

German rearmament is announced thus, and the students are excited. They are, of course, draft age. Once they might have requested ministerial deferment or a chaplain's appointment on ordination. But now they are identified with the Confessing Church so they can expect no such consideration. Bonhoeffer begins to talk about the pacifism that has so long moved on his conscience. The students are more puzzled and disturbed by that kind of talk than by the rearmament announcement. It is hard for them to see what religious strictures have to do with as political an affair as national defense.

Another night, Bonhoeffer reports the resignation of Karl Barth from the University of Bonn and his departure from Germany. His exit is forced by his refusal to sign the required oath of allegiance to Hitler. Again, some students cannot see where the problem is. Any loyal citizen or functionary ought to be loyal to the head of state, surely? But most understand that the present issue is more nuanced than that. Barth, as it happens, had declared his willingness to sign the oath if it were limited to political fealty. But he fought the oath to the nation's highest court in order to get a ruling on whether the oath was so limited. When the prevailing judicial opinion was that the oath also bound the private conscience to the Führer as ultimate lord, Barth was ready to go (especially since, to his disappointment, the Confessing Church did not ask him to take a chance and stay) and, indeed, now *has* to go. Barth himself, it became known much later, began to wonder at this time whether his own earlier counsel to the church to mind its own theological business "as if nothing were happening" were really the best he could have offered. Bonhoeffer's impatience with exactly that had been rebuked in Bonn four years before. He happened now to be doing his best to abide by Barth's earlier advice, but he was more impatient than ever.

Then comes the night when Bonhoeffer returns early, moves around the living room, plays someone's difficult bridge hand, makes a new move in a serial chess game he is always at with another crack chess player in the group, and only finally asks everyone's attention for an announcement. Niemöller has that afternoon given him advance word that on December 2, 1935, the Confessing Church will be declared illegal. From that day on, if they continue as a seminary, they will be clandestine. And since the church for which they are preparing themselves will now be an underground operation, their continued support is in question. Silence, then furor. Bonhoeffer lets the separate excited colloquies go on, then puts it to the students. He will stay as long as there is anyone to stay with him, or until the government boards up the house, and then he will look for other ways. Each man must now make up his own mind about what he will do. Bonhoeffer signals Bethge to join him, and they leave, grabbing coats on the way.

Outside, Dietrich is not so self-possessed. He tells Eberhard that that afternoon he has seen

Hannah to tell her what is coming and to make her see that if the students are willing to go on in the new danger, he will have to cut all other bonds, exist for the community. Nor would he marry now and bring any bride into such peril. She has understood. So the students' decision means more to Bonhoeffer than any of them will ever know.

The young men come to find him in the snowy yard. Rott and Koch step forward. They will all stay, of course. If Bonhoeffer's eyes shine in moonlight or windowlight, this is the most ambiguous silver ever: gratitude, pride, anxiety. Excitement.

New friends make themselves known. Matriarch Ruth von Kleist-Retzow comes over from her nearby estates and becomes a regular member of the Finkenwalde Sunday congregation. She brings her son, Hans Jurgen, and Ewald von Kleist-Schmenzin, distinguished, well-established land holders, and a friend of Ewald, Fabian von Schlabrendorff. Together the new friends hold a reception for sympathetic neighbors at the Retzow estate, where Bonhoeffer discusses the seminary and its needs. Money is pledged. Ruth von Kleist and her sons send over fruit and vegetables, cattle, chickens. That part of the future is secured.

Ruth von Kleist also sends over two teen-age grandsons to be tutored for their confirmation by

the grateful young Dr. Bonhoeffer. He is glad for
another chance at his forte, and things go so well
that grandmother brings over a twelve-year-old
granddaughter, Maria von Wedemeyer, to give her
the benefit of the same teaching. Bonhoeffer and
the boys are surprised at a slashing game of table
tennis—grandmother may be even more surprised
—but Bonhoeffer agrees to talk to Maria to see
if she is ready for the little class. She is not, and
Bonhoeffer is definite about that. Frau von Kleist
is not amused. Maria is delighted. She joins Bonhoeffer at doubles, instead.

Meanwhile, Martin Niemöller and Otto Dibelius have edited and published a massive protest
against the outlawing of the Confessing Church.
At great cost and difficulty they have had it
printed and distributed to bookstores and news-
stands. Now word comes to Finkenwalde from
Hildebrandt that the police in Berlin are systematically seizing the protest in the shops and destroying it. The seminarians galvanize. By car,
bike, motorcycle, horse, local train they spread
out through Pomerania, buying up the protest,
sometimes walking in past the police to do so,
each man buying just a copy or two where available, then cluing his accomplices to where they
should shop, too. Clothes are swapped, postures
change, and a very few youths engineer repeated
runs on the stocks of startled but delighted shop-

keepers. Toppling stacks of protests fill the halls back at Finkenwalde, until a wrapping and mailing operation gets the brochures distributed far more widely through all Germany than the sale ever would have.

Two somber, small episodes cap the exhilaration. The government, in absolute control of the state church, announces that much of the church governing in Germany will now be done by committees, on which some churchmen friendly to the Confessing Church will sit. The appeal is for all ministers to take advantage of the conciliatory disposition and come back to the state church. One student goes. The agitation of the protest campaign, the attraction of regularity in the legal church, the hope of working toward Confessing Church ends even in the state church —all these enter the agonies of his decision, as do Bonhoeffer and the students. But he goes, the only seminarian to leave the community, and anger smudges sorrow.

Then the magnificent Grandmother Bonhoeffer dies in Berlin. Dietrich has the funeral, of course. At the rites, a cousin ostentatiously refuses to shake his hand. A muttered word about "radical preachers" may make the meaning of the slight more than clear. Dietrich's funeral meditation is an expression of the family's gratitude to the great lady and to her generation. He ends it with low voice but tremulous force: *Her world* doesn't *sink into the grave with her.*

February 4, 1936, is Bonhoeffer's thirtieth birthday. The decade days have their own vertigo. Thirty had always seemed infinities off, and now forty was unimaginable. In fact, as he tells the party emphatically, that is a creaky date he does not even want to get to. The whole company is gathered around the Spanish brazier for a kind of barbecue supper. No gifts have been brought, because the boys want their young mentor to give *them* what he wants for his birthday. Plenty of badinage about that, while Bonhoeffer, surprised but obviously pleased by the twist, thinks hard.

His suggestion, when it comes, is a stunner. He wants a trip to Sweden. Yes, some of the boys knew about that; he wants to make sure the Scandinavian churches understand what the church fight is about in Germany. *That is part of it, of course,* admits Bonhoeffer, *part of the old idea. The other part of the old idea is that I want a few days in Scandinavia again, in the free air. And the new part, the birthday part? I want all of you with me, all the way.*

Pandemonium. Disbelief. It can never be done. All illegal seminary with its suspect teacher, leaving the country together? Leaving the country at all? Bonhoeffer admits it is unlikely, but so is his solo trip. Why not try? If there is any hope then everything must be done swiftly, quietly, legally. The only chance is that routine requests put in to government and national church offices may get routine handling by under officers who do not recognize suspicious names. And that is the way it is done. Contests for the most dead-pan students determine the actual applicants. Uninformative forms are submitted. And three weeks later permission is granted! New pandemonium. They must get away before reconsiderations begin. Two days later (March 1, 1936), they are in Copenhagen. Charming city, dear people—oh so knowing churchmen. It is perfectly clear to the Danes what is up in Germany. They are completely for the Confessing Church. So is Bishop Eidem in Uppsala, when they get to that ancient cathedral town in Sweden.

By this time, back in Berlin, Bishop Heckel has discovered the Finkenwalders' departure for Sweden. Anxiety heats quickly to fury. On the seminarians' arrival in shining Stockholm a Swedish newspaper does a feature article about them, referring to them as "persecuted in their own land." Heckel is in trouble. Duped by his underlings, berated by his superiors, he is beside himself.

Especially when he hears that the royal princes, Bernadotte and Eugen, are that day entertaining Bonhoeffer and his troupe, Prince Eugen especially welcoming them to his own famous art collection. The irrepressible Bonhoeffer responds by bending the royal ears about the true situation in Germany. The foreign affairs office in Berlin clues in the German ambassador in Stockholm in time for him to observe distastefully this negative diplomacy at its charming best. Heckel, too, hears from the foreign affairs office, of course.

When the group returns to Germany on March 10, the Gestapo man at the border is making a new note in the Bonhoeffer file. And then, a little later, Heckel informs church officials that *Privadozent* Dietrich Bonhoeffer has been removed from the faculty of the University of Berlin as "a pacifist and an enemy of the state," to whom no German student should again be exposed. Thus Bonhoeffer's lecture of February 14, 1936, given just before the Swedish trip, turns out to have been his last on the university faculty. Coincidentally, his father retired from the faculty, having come to retirement age, and his brother-in-law, Gerhard Leibolz, was forcibly emerited from his professorship (only thirty-four, but Jewish) at Göttingen, all in the same month with Dietrich's dismissal. Suddenly, of that whole university family, only Karl Friedrich Bonhoeffer, is on a faculty anywhere (Leipzig).

There would be a wry little fillip in one scene from an ecumenical conference in Chamby, Switzerland, in August of the same year. Heckel is there as an official representative of the German state church. Bonhoeffer, a youth officer in the ecumenical organization, is there to report on ecumenical youth activities in the past year. If the presiding officer should make the mistake of introducing Bonhoeffer as *privatdozent* at the University of Berlin, Heckel would have the pleasure of shaking his head ever so slightly, just for Bonhoeffer's sake. But then Bonhoeffer making his report, could include in it a matter of fact account of a recent Scandinavian tour by a student group from northern Germany, which had had much to tell its Swedish and Danish brothers. Happy little applause from all the isn't-youth-wonderful? and all-we-have-to-do-is-get-together group, the professionally benign. Dry satisfaction at the podium; sour twisting down below.

The crises pile up. Even events with which Bonhoeffer has little or nothing to do, leave black marks in his file. So, when Confessing Church pastors, Niemöller and Hildebrandt among them, decide to take Hitler seriously on his declared intent to keep an open mind on the church issue and address a "white paper" to him, Bonhoeffer does not happen to be among those signing the document. Yet in the stormy sequel he shares the blame. For no answer comes from Hitler. Hildebrandt frets over the delay, with Bonhoeffer. The letter to Hitler had been very frank, detailing the signers' problems with the regime, and not just in its church activities. Questions were asked about compulsory hatred of Jews, encouragement of spying, falsification of votes, oath requirements. Nervousness grows. Only three copies of the white paper had been made, in hope that absence of publicity would give the Führer a chance to make confidential answer. Hitler had one copy, another was sealed in the safekeeping of a trusted Swede, the third was locked up by Friedrich Weissler, lawyer for the Confessing Church.

Then, six weeks after the white paper was submitted, it is carried in all its damaging explicitness in London and Basle newspapers (in July, 1936, the rest of the world had hardly begun to make up its mind about Germany). The white paper's careful questions came as confirmation of the worst rumors floating then in world capitals. Official chicanery, inhuman repressions, genocidal tendencies in Berlin were more than implied in the clergymen's document. The terribly imperiled Confessing Churchmen are frantic. Who could have jeopardized them so carelessly? Surely for the only time in all those upside down years, the Confessing Church appeals to the Gestapo to find the culprits! The separate Lutheran churches at once further disassociate themselves from the pariah Confessors, who are themselves distraught at finding their solemn, loyal warning and appeal thus suddenly turned into foreign propaganda.

No one knows who the culprit is. Consternation rages in all conversations. Bonhoeffer stays out of it, though. He is sure he knows who the culprits are: Ernst Tillich, a student of his at the university and a companion at the Fanø conference, and Werner Koch, a favorite Finkenwalder, and a comrade on trips both to Switzerland and to Sweden.

These sharp young men had "borrowed" the copy of the white paper controlled by Weissler. They copied it verbatim, overnight, and returned it to the lawyer. Might Bonhoeffer have found them copying the document? Or did they soon show him their copy? However it was, he seems to have been the only one not involved who knew there was a fourth copy in youthful, enthusiastic, impatient hands. The boys went into independent action only after Hitler's long silence and after it became clear the Confessing Church was not going to release its fruitless text.

Tillich and Weissler are arrested in October, Koch in November. In February, 1937, all three are sent to the concentration camp at Sacksenhausen where the Jewish Weissler dies in torture six days later. (Koch is released two years later, Tillich three.) If the Gestapo had missed the younger men's connection with Bonhoeffer before (the Gestapo had not), it does not afterwards. Bonhoeffer stays close to Koch, especially, throughout, collecting black marks for visits, letters, gifts to the prisoner.

There are other colleagues to write and visit in jail too. In these months more and more pastors are being arrested, and friends are fleeing. Bonhoeffer uses his London connections to get many to England. He even has to give up Bethge for a few months when one of the churches asks the young Saxon to fill in for an arrested minister. Bonhoeffer yields on that with little grace, asking that it not be made a habit—though such emergency relief was one of the declared purposes of the Finkenwalde community.

At the community, life does go on, in spite of all the surrounding turmoil. The young men are now pushing "missions" to neighboring parishes. Four by four they go out on their tours, visiting in the homes, holding classes for children, conducting services on Sunday—preaching forty-minute sermons, ten minutes per man. They bring back reports of dead churches. Nobody comes to services, the farmers will not talk to people they suspect of being liberal, the children's classes go from fifteen (out of the forty-four available in one parish) in a first session, to three in the next, because, it turns out, the first lesson was on the Old Testament prophets and they are Jews. Then the various town authorities take to confiscating the "missionaries'" collections and the police office forces them all to register.

New arrests, new flights, the missionary miseries—all are reported to Bonhoeffer at Finkenwalde, where the lectures still are delivered, music somehow goes on, swimming continues; tickets to the Olympic Games are purchased for everyone by Bonhoeffer, two boys who have never flown before go to Berlin by air—and the sick are joyfully dosed back to health by the pill-happy director.

Three short episodes repeat long familiar, positive themes, but this time all are played in the minor. Travel, for instance, takes Dietrich and Eberhard (on brief vacation) to Italy. Under enthusiastic, knowing guidance, Bethge does Rome, especially St. Peter's. All the old joy is in the form and in the fact of the travel. But the blight on all the brightness of these years will show itself, without comment, when the young men are pictured on a crowded street corner, cut off from the Colosseum by Mussolini's battalions marching in from their Abyssinian triumph.

The family gathers in Berlin for Mrs. Bonhoeffer's sixtieth birthday. All the children are there: Karl Friedrich (who has by now given up his heavy-water experiments) and Greta; Klaus (who is a chief lawyer for Lufthansa) and Emmi; Ursula and Rüdiger Schleicher, from next door; Christine and Hans von Dohnanyi, who have seen more and more of Dietrich lately, in Berlin and in Finkenwalde; Sabine and Gerhard Leibholz, who are at loose ends, do not know quite what to do; and young Suzanne and Walter Dress. A tasteful but hilarious performance of Hayden's "Toy Symphony" is rehearsed by the grandchildren in the Schleicher's music room, then performed for the grandmother at her party. It is, in fact, the last time that the whole family will be together. No one can know that at the time, of course, but while the fatally bound four—Klaus, Rüdiger, Hans, Dietrich—make some kind of music together, it is not inconceivable that the two youngest sisters might confess to each other their anxiety about future reunions.

Dietrich closes out his ecumenical participation a month later (February, 1937). A week in London at committee meetings will turn out to be his last official action in that movement. From now on his ecumenical connections will be personal and private.

Now the government gets tougher. There is a new wave of arrests among Confessing Church pastors. The Finkenwalde student body is sharply reduced; Wilhelm Rott, Bonhoeffer's assistant, is arrested (by Christmas, 1937, twenty-seven of the students and alumni will be in jail). No more passports or exit permits are given the ministers.

June 16, 1937, Wilhelm Niesel is arrested. His trial is set for July 2, so on July 1, Dietrich Bonhoeffer returns to Berlin to be on hand. He and Bethge go late in the morning to consult with Martin Niemöller. Dr. Niemöller is not at home, but Mrs. Niemöller invites the worried young churchmen in to join Hildebrandt, his assistant, also waiting for her husband. They are barely settled when a frantic minister (Eugen Rose, who was on the Swedish trip) pounds on the door and bursts in before anyone can respond. Martin Niemöller has just been arrested at church head-quarters. The shattering news is hardly out be-fore the police fleet of big black Mercedes-Benz limousines is parking in front of the house. Mrs. Niemöller, Hildebrandt, Bonhoeffer, Bethge, and Rose race for the back door of the house. When they wrench it open, the police are there.

For eight hours the little group is under house arrest. Another friend arrives, and he, too, is locked in. The police take all telephone calls. No news gets out or in. Thirty thousand marks col-lected for the Confessing Church are found in a wall safe and confiscated. The only humor in the situation is in the fascination of the youthful ministers with the impeccable order of Niemöl-ler's sermon manuscripts—in the thorough search by the police these homiletical files are uncovered and the men have a hard time relating such secret system to their tempermental, impulsive senior.

There is one other quirky bit. In midafter-noon, Franz, looking anxiously out the front window, wonders *who* can be watching the house from the chauffeured black limousine that he notes repeatedly passing. Later, Dietrich, standing by the window, wonders apropos of nothing how his mother could have found out he was in trouble. Everyone reassures him that she could not possibly know, will not have to be worried about him at all since he can tell her all about it himself when they are released later. *But that was my mother who just passed in that big black car*, he observes. *Big black car*, Franz exclaims, *why then she has been going by for hours!*

As soon as they are released, Bonhoeffer and Bethge rally the Finkenwalders to a protest demonstration in the street before Niemöller's church. The police wade in, arrest 250 demonstrators, including more Finkenwalders. Hildebrandt takes over Niemöller's pulpit and lasts two weeks. On both Sundays he asks for a collection for the illegal Confessing Church and prays for a long list of imprisoned Confessing Church pastors. He is arrested. Many friends, including the Bonhoeffers, go to work on his behalf. Four weeks later he is released and goes at once to London.

Bonhoeffer and Bethge are not at Finkenwalde when the end comes there. In end-of-term break (September, 1937) they are visiting the Leibholzes at Göttingen when word comes from the seminary's frightened and indignant housekeeper. The Gestapo has boarded up the school. As the friends proceed to Berlin they are blocked on their way to the Bonhoeffer house by the parade heralding Mussolini's arrival in Hitler's capital. Wilhelm Rott is released from prison about then, and Bonhoeffer arranges the celebration: All three go to hear "*Don Giovanni*." Doctrine may call on one to do or die for Last Things only; but in practice, first things first.

Conspiracy

The story more and more tells itself. The conceptual struggle which up to now has had to be read between the lines and pieced together and related to the action, now declares itself in events. The long effort to serve and affect the world's health by working for the church's purity, the obedient effort to read the earth through heaven, to minimize immediate interests and to concentrate on ultimate ends runs down.

Typically, the conceptual crisis in Bonhoeffer is sparked by no big ideational collisions. It is forced by hard facts in the world he cares most about. His twin sister and her husband have to flee Germany. He himself has to register for the draft. Inhumanity, horror, war are here. All the church's valiance has been unavailing. This is not medieval Europe; the spoilers of the modern world do not grapple with a giant when they take on the church, they slap at a gnat. There must be something more for a Christian to do than keeping gnat nuisances buzzing purely? Especially gnats that then lose their nerve?

Through his family he meets men and women who have never been hung up for a moment on the technical questions of theological ultimacy but who are now risking everything to save human life and its decency, Bonhoeffer's own tacitly revered penultimacies. He throws in with these heroes of the here and now. He throws in his comfort and his preference, he throws away an easy out, he throws off pacifistic inhibitions. He takes long second looks at his earlier ideas. He breaks out of "the enchantment of the ultimate" (Eberbard Bethge) and comes down much stronger for "the Things Before the Last" than he would have once. When he has to take off on a dangerous international trip for the Resistance, he leaves unfinished an essay in which he was establishing the basic importance of "the natural."

But now he does not wait for preliminary doctrinal justification for what he does. This time *what he does will help him see how things really are*. So we arrive at the Bonhoeffer who one generation ago anticipated our presently active generation and its whole habit of thought.

STORY VI

The end of Finkenwalde is not the end of ministerial education for the Confessing Church. The clandestine operation is just further diversified and decentralized. Two remote parishes, Kösslin and Schlawe, are located and each is assigned seven to ten young assistant pastors. Bonhoeffer and Bethge live in the Schlawe parish, and register with the police there as assistant pastors. The Schlawe contingent lives in Sigurdhof, the last house in town. It is in the forest, beside a bright stream, and features no electricity, much pumping, and candles at night. Still deeper in the forest is a hunting lodge, available when snoopers might wonder at the number of military age civilians living in one house. Trust Bonhoeffer, though. On the run they might be, but on the way they ski and skate, boat, and play tennis at a neighboring castle!

Twice a week Assistant Pastor Bonhoeffer drives his new Mercedes or his motorcycle sixty kilometers to hold unpublicized, even camouflaged classes (Christology told like a secret, heads together in a beer hall? ecclesiology in a volleyball game?) with his "assistant pastor" colleagues in Kösslin. The same courses are given, of course, to the Schlawe companions. And always there are the visits to Berlin. Dietrich still brings back the news, but the students around this time begin to think that he may not be telling all he knows. They do not take this personally. They sense that he is developing another life alongside the one they share. But the competition is not between them and someone else; it is between the church and something else. . . .

January 11, 1938, Bonhoeffer is arrested with eleven others at a church meeting in Berlin. He is not imprisoned, but the Gestapo puts him on a train to Schlawe. This time the note in his file forbids his returning to Berlin. Berlin is now off-limits to Bonhoeffer. Back in Schlawe he and the students ransack their own desks and effects for *anything* that might incriminate themselves or anyone else when, as they are sure they will be, they are searched.

In June there is a reunion of old Finkenwalders in Zingst, where it all began. Their good time is the only happiness in the whole church this summer. The government is tracking down everyone who has not yet signed the oath of absolute allegiance to the Führer. To Bonhoeffer's shame, the pastors are capitulating. The fact that his father has wrangled permission for him to *visit* in Berlin whenever he wants is some help, but there is no escaping the fact that the church to which he had given his time and his attention, the church for which he had taken chances, the church which he had accepted as *the* arena for Christian resistance, is knuckling under.

Sometime in these days, Hans von Dohnanyi (for his own serious reasons) asks Dietrich what Jesus meant with his claim that "he who takes up the sword shall die by the sword." And Dietrich, knowing something of what lies behind the question (guessing something of what lies ahead?) says: It means what it says. As I and my pacifist friends teach, it is a prohibition. But sometimes. . . . sometimes it may be simply a realistic appraisal for men who *should* take up the sword.

For the world is coming on stronger than ever. On September 9, 1938, Hans von Dohnanyi gets word to Dietrich that new measures against the Jews are being prepared by the government. Dr. and Mrs. Bonhoeffer communicate with the Leibholzes and help with their arrangements. Dietrich and Eberhard go to Göttingen, accompany the Leibholzes as far as Giessen, desperate to put a happy picnic facade on the whole dangerous strategem. There Dietrich waves goodbye to his twin and her family. By midnight they have talked their way across the border at Basle. A month later, by edict of the state, all Jewish men's passports have to be stamped with a "J," all Jewish women's with an "S." Calmly, and speaking of hope the grieving senior Bonhoeffers call Switzerland to urge the Leibholzes not to return (instead they go to England where, at Chichester's suggestion, Gerhard is invited to join the Oxford faculty).

The invasion of Czechoslovakia is bruited. Then, November 3, 1938, German youth is required to register for the draft. Bonhoeffer registers in Schlawe, counting on his friends in that small place to protect his interests as well as possible. He does not know himself, at this time, exactly what those interests might be. He cannot imagine fighting in the troops; he is not sure he is ready to declare himself a conscientious objector; he knows that his beleagured church does not want him to be tried for military evasion, thus creating a new issue between church and state. What he wants is time.

November 9, 1938, is *Kristallnacht*, the night of the desecration and destruction of synagogues and Jewish-owned shops all over Germany. It might as well be that night that Hans and Christine von Dohnanyi explain to Dietrich the depth of the conspiracy in which Dietrich has more or less known they were involved—and the depth of their involvement.

There are two Secret Services in Nazi Germany: the Gestapo, responsible for political intelligence; and the Abwehr, responsible for military intelligence. Each is interested in the other, of course, jealous and critical. Each is eager to get what it can on the other. In the Abwehr there is, as a matter of fact, one unit almost completely preoccupied with political intelligence. Admiral Canaris, head of the Abwehr, knows about this unit, of course, and what its secret purpose is. Under Colonel Oster this unit is to plot the removal or death of Adolf Hitler. Admiral Canaris created the unit for that purpose, with the approval of the greatly distinguished General Ludwig Beck, Chief of the General Staff. Colonel Oster's principal officer in this plot is Hans von Dohnanyi. Hans has been keeping a careful chronicle of the whole scandal of Nazi governance. The documented horror is beyond Dietrich's anticipation or comprehension.

The discussion could move to the increasing possibility of Dietrich's being drafted. There is a little talk about his leaving the country again for a while. Then Christine could point out, carefully, that if Dietrich were working with the Abwehr, he would of course be given draft exemption. Dietrich is startled by the idea, and not noticeably attracted. He is sure by now that he is not going to fight, certainly not for Hitler, but he is not sure entering a plot is the right way for a minister to go; there must be other options. Christine understands, but wants to be understood too: *After seeing what is happening, you could stand back from resistance?* Dietrich is a little stung: *I have not hung back, and the government knows that I haven't. I have been arrested, had my school closed, been thrown out of Berlin. . . .* His forthright sister insists: *It is not enough, it is in the wrong place, it is with the wrong people; A doctrinally sure church was going to defend men, but it turns out to be a church of men defending doctrines.* Dietrich, who knows that all too well, tries another tack: *You know how I feel about killing, and this plotting has to do with murder just as the army does.* Christine is unyielding. *Of course we know how you feel about killing, Dietrich, who doesn't? But how do you feel about our Gerhard and your Franz and your Jesus and our Jews, millions of them, and Poles and Slavs and French, and your English and Americans, too, if our leader can get his murderous hands on them?* Christine never wheedles; she presses hard, crisp, lawyer-like: *Does your theology have to plug up your plain humanity? Does your Jesus keep you locked in his church? Can't you come out and just help us?*

The dialogue is meant to be forceful, but this is not an argument between the brother and sister. Each knows, feels all the pros and cons within himself. Hans is less importunate: *You have thought what was needed, Dietrich, was open, honest men taking firm stands for the right, but such knights come from earlier stories about simpler times. What we need now are flexible men*

*in strategic spots. But we will not press. As you
say, there are other options. Even if all were to
resist, only some will conspire. And even approv-
ing conspiracy leaves the question whether you
should also be a conspirator. Anyway, you know
what is going on. We need you, but you cannot be
really useful until you see our treason as your
patriotism.*

Bonhoeffer tries travel. He gives up Italian
plans, lest the special permissions needed bring
his name to the attention of draft boards.
The procedures for getting to England, though,
are more practiced, and so travel permits come
through somehow. The Confessing Church agents
are especially helpful in this: They did not want
any new fuss kicked up by a minister uncertain
of his duty.

In London there is glad reunion with the Bishop
of Chichester. And at Paddington Station one
afternoon, Bonhoeffer meets the new general
secretary of the ecumenical movement, Dr.
Willem Visser 't Hooft, on from Geneva. Walking up and down the platform, separated now and
then by crowds, lost to each other in occasional
steam blasts, the young men discover the coinci-
dences of attitude and opinion which assure Bonhoeffer that he and the Confessing Church have a
strong voice in Geneva, whether they can get out
to conferences or not.

Dietrich sees the film *Queen Victoria*, one

afternoon, and to his own surprise weeps for the old steadiness of England and the new stress he knows is coming.

Dr. Reinhold Niebuhr, a teacher of Bonhoeffer's at Union eight years before, is delivering his Gifford Lectures these months in Scotland. At the moment, though, he is vacationing in Sussex. Dietrich seeks him out there to discuss his impasse in Germany. It is a crisscrossed occasion. Here is the antimilitaristic Bonhoeffer, determined to avoid army service, seeking counsel and help from archinterventionist, antipacifist Niebuhr—who could not have been more willing to keep anybody out of Hitler's army, however contrary the philosophies.

Professor Niebuhr goes into action immediately. Paul Lehmann is contacted in Illinois, asked to set up a lecture tour in colleges and seminaries (at $25–$50!) for Bonhoeffer. President Henry Sloane Coffin at Union offers a summer teaching post. The American ecumenical leader, Henry Smith Leiper, looks into other possibilities. The Confessing Church, as eager to get its story told abroad as it is loathe to have new crises develop around Bonhoeffer at home, gives him permission to leave. The German government is satisfied that the request for extended leave is bona fide, and Dietrich is off. Karl Friedrich, on his way to a summer lectureship at the University of Chicago, sails with him.

By June 10, 1939, Dietrich Bonhoeffer is in New York City. Uneasy from the start, unsure that he should have come away at all, terribly worried about everyone and everything left behind, far from satisfied with his own solution to his German problem, his turmoil is only compounded by early developments in America.

Dr. Leiper is delighted to be able to press a chaplaincy to the German refugees on Bonhoeffer (Paul Tillich had encouraged the offer). Bonhoeffer is distraught. That would be a long-term job, and he cannot think of staying away long. Furthermore, it is the kind of job that would make it impossible for him ever to reenter Germany under its present regime.

Lonely (letters were slow from Germany), uncertain, Bonhoeffer takes to the streets on the hot night of June 19. Around and around the tawdry Times Square he goes. The headlines flashing their way around the Times Building are all about Germany; the Seventh Avenue newsreel theater he haunts shows reel after reel of reports from his country; on the streets Germanically accented English and variously accented German beat around him. Wondering and worrying about family, friends, the "assistant pastors" still meeting for classes in the clean countryside, he works his way time and again around the raunchy square and through the clots of randy youth at Broadway and Forty-Second Street.

Sometime in that night the decision is made. By next day he is telling Dr. Leiper he cannot accept the refugee chaplaincy, and writing Paul Lehmann that he cannot keep the speaking dates. There is disappointment from all, anxiety for him. But from the moment of decision, Bonhoeffer's mind clears. A few days later sitting in the garden of Dr. Coffin's home (he is dazzled by the fireflies in the evening, a novelty to Europeans, and reminded of Freidrichsbrunn by the Connecticut hills) he writes Reinhold Niebuhr about his decision:

> I have come to the conclusion that I have made a mistake in coming to America. I must live through this difficult period of our national history with the Christian people of Germany. I will have no right to participate in the reconstruction of Christian life in Germany after the war if I do not share the trials of this time with my people. . . . Such a decision each man must make for himself. Christians in Germany will face the terrible alternative of either willing the defeat of their nation in order that Christian civilization may survive, or willing the victory of their nation and thereby destroying our civilization. I know which of these alternatives I must choose; but I cannot make that choice in security. . . .

Bonhoeffer's decision to return was obviously much more than that. It may not have been clear to him then how far he would be ready to go in the Resistance; even when he was back in Germany his full participation took a while to develop. But already he could admit in his diary that he was thinking less and less about the church.

Paul Lehmann hurries to New York for a brief reunion before Bonhoeffer's departure. Karl Friedrich arrives from Chicago, where he has turned down an invitation to join the faculty at the University of Chicago. On the blistering midnight of July 7 the brothers sail for home.

It is a Great Divide, this Atlantic crossing. The movie could well begin here, flashing back as it moves forward. One kind of resistance is played out; now another will begin. In London the brothers visit Sabine and Gerhard; Uncle Dietrich teaches their children some English nursery rhymes (Humpty Dumpty is the appropriate political *double-entendre* for the film). And there Bonhoeffer hears of Pastor Paul Schneider's end, beaten to death in prison for refusing to honor Hitler. No wonder the treasured photographs taken of the twins, Dietrich and Sabine Bonhoeffer, together for the last time, show the youthful theologian assured, calm, affectionate as ever—and uncommonly pensive.

By the end of July Bonhoeffer and the other assistant pastors are celebrating their reunion at the beach. There they hear the news of the German-Russian pact, and hear the planes taking off for Poland from airfields just behind the dunes on which they sit. The current semester at Köslin and Schlawe is called off. The Confessing Church pastors are drafted in droves, and some are killed in the first days of the war. Bonhoeffer, more determined than ever to stay out of the army, applies for a military chaplaincy and is turned down. His influential friends in Schlawe manage to further delay his draft. A new semester is begun in the parsonages.

On March 18, 1940, while Bonhoeffer and Bethge are away from Schlawe, they get a call from the same harried housekeeper: The Gestapo has just appeared and shuttered both quasi dormitories, scattered the quasi students. This time no subterfuge is possible; school is out.

That night, racing their car over snow and ice, the friends drive to Berlin. The next day Hans von Dohnanyi introduces Dietrich to General Beck, General Oster, and Ulrich von Hassell, who invite him to join them in working out surrender terms for Germany. (Later developments will be well served if a Dr. Karl Sack can be included in the group, too.) It is an impossible moment. Hitler is having his most dramatic triumphs in the very hour that distinguished, high-placed officers and a young theologian consider what they should promise the enemy to whom they want to give the victory. But it is exactly the Polish successes that have moved the generals. The barbarisms and insane cruelties ordered there by Hitler separate him irrevocably from even the most strained conception of German honor. Two attempts on Hitler's life (by assailants unknown to these men) having failed, the Abwehr group of high military conspirators now hopes to arrange a capitulation which the allies might accept.

Swiftly they agree to offer a decentralized Germany (without a Führer, of course) and an immediate, neutrally safeguarded chance for Austria to vote on its own future. Lawyer Joseph Müller, (later a minister of state), Roman Catholic contact man for the Abwehr conspirators, gets the Pope's approval of the terms at once. Then General Halder takes the document to Commander-in-Chief General von Brauchitsch (who is known to be offended by Hitler's Polish orders) —who throws it back, denouncing it as treason and the work of traitors. Bonhoeffer and General Oster, at the end of the sequence, are discussing not just the close call they have had with von Brauchitsch, but the treason that is patriotism, the patriotism that is treason.

But Bonhoeffer is still not ready for the big break. The Confessing Church sends him back into church action. He is still able to preach outside Berlin, so the remaining church officers dispatch him to East Prussia. There he visits parishes, holds pastoral consultations with the faithful clergy, meets old Finkenwalders.

The change is working in him, though. It is on this trip that he and Bethge, sitting in a Memel restaurant, hear the radio news of Hitler's triumph in France (June 17, 1940). All diners leap to their feet, shouting, arms up, "*Sieg heil, heil Hitler.*" *Deutschland, deutschland, über alles* they sing, and the *Horst Wessel* song. Bethge remains seated, then notes, bewildered, that Bonhoeffer is on his feet too, saluting, singing with the rest. He tugs at Dietrich, who grates down at him, "Get up and start hollering; *this* isn't worth dying for." So both knights are now off their horses. The appearance of righteousness is no longer important. Gesture time is over. To fight entrenched evil, one must at last join "the great masquerade of evil." A visit by Bonhoeffer and Bethge to the Bamberg Cathedral (visited first in those early Wanderjahre scenes) might be the occasion for developing dialogue to this end. This time the "perfit gentil knight" will look very small to Bonhoeffer.

A second tour is undertaken. This time, at Bloestau, while he is addressing a young people's group after a regular service, the Gestapo abruptly breaks up the meeting. It may have been a routine gesture; Bonhoeffer thought it was aimed at him. By the time he gets to the Latvian border (Russia was cutting across Latvia, those days) he has had enough of this resistance at one remove.

He returns to Berlin, and apparently volunteers for Abwehr service. Technically he is now a secret agent of the Hitler government! Actually, he is a part of the anti-Hitler conspiracy. The Abwehr asks him first to return to the eastern front, under the guise of his interrupted preaching mission. The conspirators know that Hitler is planning a great betrayal of the Russians; Oster wants to know what is going on near the border.

So shortly Bonhoeffer is back in Königsberg. Only this time he checks in not just with churchmen but with the Abwehr agents in the area, on whose protection he will depend, if necessary. At the same time he stops keeping a diary.

Suddenly a call comes from the police in the Schlawe area, where he is registered. But it is not the draft, as he feared on his way there. Instead, the Gestapo informs him that he is from that date forbidden to preach or lecture again anywhere in Germany. Furthermore, he must now register all his movements, reporting immediately to the police whenever he changes locality. As he leaves the station Dietrich becomes aware of the Gestapo surveillance he will never again be without. For a while he gives them little exertion. He settles down in Klein-Krössin for about a month and works on the first chapter of the (posthumously published) *Ethics*. It was to be as much an understanding of his action already begun as a base for action to come.

The church does not know quite what to do with its now marked minister. There is talk of sending him to a minuscule parish in tiny Bismark. While the leaders deliberate, Bonhoeffer goes to Berlin and enters the Abwehr service. Oster gets him immediate military exemption as "indispensable to the government's secret service." Bonhoeffer asks Dohnanyi to do the same for as many of the Confessing Church pastors as possible, pleading the importance the Abwehr places on normalization of community life. Many

pastors (including Niesel) are so excused, thanks
to Dohnanyi's efforts.

But the Abwehr is worried about the Gestapo
surveillance of their newest agent, and especially by the requirement that he register all his
movements. The last thing they need is a legal
excuse for the Gestapo to come checking up on
anyone in the Abwehr central office. So Bonhoeffer is assigned to the Munich office. There he es-
tablishes legal residence with his aunt, the Countess Kalkreuth. Actually, thanks to his coconspir-
ator, Josef Müller, he will spend most of his time
at the Kloster (monastery) Ettal in the mountains south of Munich (where he is amused but
delighted to hear the monk-of-the-day reading
from the Bonhoeffer *Cost of Discipleship* for the
lunching monks in their commons!)

He is at Ettal, one day, working on his *Ethics*,
when the Countess Kalkreuth telephones anxiously to say the Gestapo has inquired for him and
asked her to "get him here at once." The confrontation is anticlimactic. The brusque officers
want only to inform him that the requirement
that he register his movements has been voided.

* * *

So the strange double life develops its own
ambiguous style. For weeks in a row he lives at
snowy Ettal, working on his new *Ethics* in the
old library; in other weeks he visits his old bene-
factress, Ruth von Kleist-Retzow, at her Klein-
Krössin estates. There too he writes ethics. Every

chapter, as it is sketched, brings him farther into the new theological country his new political activity is showing him. Christ is more the center of the thinking than ever, but now a Christ whose dominion spreads far beyond individual and church into society, state, politics, institutions, and who is most directly served in the practical world. The old "penultimates," to which he has always been so natively sensitive, begin to find in his theology the authority they have always had in his life. Nothing is finished, much is merely sketched, even his own implications are only partly seen, but the mind that had already marched so independently on familiar ground now is on its way into novelty.

Other days he is at the family home in Berlin, back at the quartet evenings with conspiratorial cronies, or playing piano-violin sonatas (Mozart, Beethoven, Brahms) with Rüdiger Schleicher next door. Such nights generally ended with quiet, excited talk about national developments, Dietrich always ranging himself with the optimistic plotters, spinning hopeful interpretations of events, making big plans, while Hans von Dohnanyi remains cautious, skeptical, careful. Similar meetings at Ettal bring Dietrich and Hans together regularly with Josef Müller and other Roman Catholic resisters.

Early in 1941 the optimists look like the realists in the crowd. England refuses to buckle, Roosevelt is installed in his third term, Greece stops Italy, German invasions either to east or west are delayed. The conspiracy contacts von Brauchitsch again and finds him less touchy. Larger cooperation apparently depends upon some assurance that the Allies will be willing to treat constructively with a new, anti-Fascist German government if the highest ranking officers were to join the conspiracy to remove Hitler and set up such a government.

Dietrich Bonhoeffer is sent to Switzerland to give cautious word in the right quarters about the Resistance to see if his old ecumenical and English contacts will help put the plotters and the Allied governments in confidential communication with each other. The Abwehr credentials Bonhoeffer carries get him across the German border easily, but they are hardly the most reassuring papers he could have presented to the Swiss frontier guards. For a while there is real question of his admission. Then he asks permission to call Professor Karl Barth in Basle, now world-famous for his anti-Hitler activities. Dr. Barth reassures the border patrol about Bonhoeffer, and he is admitted. But Barth is worried, privately, about what his mercurial young friend is up to as an agent for the Hitler government. In the madness of these years, unthinkables had a terrible way of turning into facts. Four weeks in Zurich and Geneva put Bonhoeffer back in touch with the men and offices through whom the Resistance hoped to work. Facts about the Resistance are given guardedly; they are certified in Switzerland by Bonhoeffer's own earlier well-known identification with ecu-

menical peace efforts. The channels the conspirators need are open. On his return, Bonhoeffer
stops in Basle to see the puzzled Barth. To him,
Dietrich discloses everything he knows about the
conspiracy.

Back in Munich, Bonhoeffer is informed by the
Gestapo that he is now forbidden to write or
publish anything. The order is a general one,
covering others besides Bonhoeffer, but he could
hardly believe, considering its timing, it was not
designed principally for himself, the elusive
strangely mobile scholar.

Easter, 1941, is spent at the childhood country
home, Friedrichsbrunn. The summer is divided
between Klein-Krössin, Berlin, and Munich. The
writing goes forward (Bonhoeffer had never expected to be able to publish it in Hitler's Germany), becoming more and more polemical, an
ethics testing itself always on the issues upper-
most at the moment: racial theories, leadership
principles, national destiny, euthanasia, genocide,
abortion, suicide.

It would seem a bad season for conspiracy.
Hitler's armies are rampaging through Russia.
But when the Führer declares open season on
civilians, his officers are horrified. The chiefs of
staff seek disassociation from the SS murderers
(this is the point of Bishop Heckel's final disen-
chantment). But the victories, as they pile up,
buttress Hitler's authority, and his removal to

the impregnable "Wolf's Lair" puts him out of physical reach.

The conspiracy tries to act, anyway. Once again (September, 1941) Bonhoeffer is off to Geneva. He is himself so sure that the end is near that he walks into Dr. Visser 't Hooft's office saying, *Well, it's all over, isn't it?* The ecumenical official can not believe what he has heard: *You mean, Germany has won?*

But no, I mean Hitler is through. The conspirators are ready to go. The men around Hitler whom they must involve if they are to get to Hitler at all ask only the hope of such terms from the Allies as will give a new government a chance to survive, should it prevail. They do not ask assurance, but will be nerved by any indication that Hitler and Germany as a whole are not inextricably combined in the thinking of Allied statesmen, and that peace aims of order and justice for all of Europe are their larger ends. Bonhoeffer gets that word going through channels to Allied capitals. Along with it goes every indication he can safely give of the size and resolution of the Resistance. This is meant especially for the English who could not believe that there was any such movement high enough in the government to be taken seriously (Winston Churchill had growled to Ewald von Kleist, "Bring me Hitler's head, and we can talk about the rest").

Only at the end of this month-long visit (Bonhoeffer saw Sutz, visited friends on the Zurichsee, worked on *Ethics* there) does Dietrich's ebullience fade. In a last call on Visser 't Hooft, he crumples: *Now we must pray for the defeat of my country.*

But Bonhoeffer himself has not waited till now to begin that terrible service for Germany.

Back at his parents' home in Berlin, Bonhoeffer is ill and convalescing for most of the next three months (October–December). Nothing in the nation encourages health. The euthanasia measures are being publicly pressed. Jews, recently ordered to wear yellow stars on their sleeves, are now being picked up and trucked away. As rumors grow thicker and sicker, Bonhoeffer gets up to go with Friedrick Justus Perels, his friend from Finkenwalde days, to Cologne, Dusseldorf, and Eberfeld, collecting information on the genocide now under way. Their horrified and furious analysis is given to the Resistance in hope that the military can be persuaded to intervene. (The Bonhoeffer–Perels paper is the first conspiracy's documentation of this Nazi crime.) The Confessing Church, fighting for its own flickering life now, makes a few, unavailing protests.

Meanwhile, Jewish friends and neighbors are calling at the Bonhoeffer and Schleicher homes. Dietrich and Hans are shortly involved in what came to be called the U-7 plot. Originally, seven Jewish associates were to be smuggled out of Germany, but finally more are included. The whole scheme takes months to bring off. Gestapo approval has to be gained, somehow, and while that is being wangled, the names of the escaping men and women must be removed over and over again, one way or another, from the regularly new lists of Jews to be transported to concentration camps. Then the Swiss churchmen who are to receive the refugees have trouble getting permission from their government for the secret transaction. Bonhoeffer calls Professor Barth, again, and permission comes. But (it is still standard practice) without work permits. So money has to be raised, enough to guarantee the support of the whole group. Hans von Dohnanyi is especially resourceful in that campaign.

Dr. Bethge details the last afternoon in Germany of one of the refugees, Charlotte Friedenthal. She had to go to the Gestapo for a final permit. She knew she would be required to wear her yellow star in the office. But how to get there in time? Public transportation was off-limits to Jews. So she took off her coat and carried it rolled up as she took a streetcar. Getting off one block before the Gestapo office, she was able to get back into her coat and star before she presented herself. Next, to the Swiss consulate. There the star was unnecessary so she took it off her coat. Hans called for her at her home shortly, to take her to the station. Stupid to take risks this late in the adventure, so at his suggestion Miss Friedenthal sewed the cursed star back on. In her compartment on the train she simply rolled up her ill-starred coat again and used it as a pillow. Getting chilly, near the border, she finally put it on—to the contempt and indignation of the only other passenger left in her compartment. At the border, German agents took all her papers and disappeared. But after a while they returned and put her across the border. The Swiss who welcomed her insisted she remove the blasphemous star at once.

Now Hans heartens the slowly mending but heartsick Bonhoeffer with word that General von Brauchitsch has at last given his word that though he cannot join the various conspiracies he will not betray them, nor will he interfere with their success. His disposition is, of course, crucially important. As commander of the armies, he would be in a position to order a smooth take-over of the government if the conspirators could take care of Hitler. The good news is hardly heard before the radio brings later word: Hitler has just removed von Brauchitsch and will now himself take over the whole military exercise.

The disappointment has to do with more than the immediate issue. The new announcement means that the Abwehr's whole strategy, to get the military leadership to lead an intact nation into negotiations with the Allies for a stable Europe, is doomed. Hitler is now his own military leadership. A strike from the top is no longer possible. So everything has to be done over again. Assassination is the only possibility. While new plots are being laid, Bonhoeffer asks to be included among those who would shoot the dictator if called upon, asking time only to resign from the church first. Even in the terror and agony of their decision, the coconspirators know this is a ludicrous idea. As Hans points out, gently, only a military man can now get within shooting distance of the barricaded tyrant—and anyway, Dietrich would not know which end of a gun to hold. But no one laughs. Bonhoeffer's pacifistic leanings are well known. Abruptly the little group realizes what precious sacrifice the young preacher is willing to make.

Sometime in the spring of 1942, Hans von Dohnanyi realizes that the Gestapo has tapped his phone, is reading his mail.

Bonhoeffer returns to action in connection with a Norwegian crisis. The Nazi-sponsored Quisling's accession to power there in February 1942 settled nothing in that occupied country. Resistance was widespread, strong, elusive. In this the Norwegian church was a ringleader. Infuriated, Quisling government authorities barred Dean Fjellbu from his Trondheim cathedral. At once all Norwegian bishops announced suspension of any activity that might directly serve the state. Then one thousand teachers resigned from the Norwegian schools rather than lead their pupils into a Norwegian Hitler youth organization. On Easter Sunday all Norwegian pastors resigned. Next day Bishop Eivind Berggrav was placed under house arrest, then imprisoned. As per prearrangement, a German transport officer stationed in Norway at once cables his colleague in another homeland conspiritorial group (the Kreisau), Count Helmut von Moltke, telling him of Berggrav's arrest. Moltke informs the Abwehr, and the Abwehr sends Moltke and Bonhoeffer to investigate.

By April 10, the two "investigators" are cabling back the preconceived advice. For the sake of order in the occupied country, Bishop Berggrav must be released at once. On April 15 Martin Bormann sends the order to release the bishop but to keep him away from Oslo. And all the time he is in Norway, Bonhoeffer is urging every Norwegian he can get next to not to let up the pressure! Do not give an inch. Be a nuisance. Hold the line.

Bonhoeffer could hardly have been human— and he was abundantly that—if he did not have at least a few I-told-you-so feelings in Norway. The Norwegian ministers' strikes were precisely what he and Hildebrandt had begged for in Berlin in 1933 when such parabolic action might still have meant much there. The suggested strikes were called unrealistic then; now their effectiveness became clear.

The eminently human Bonhoeffer sees to it that the trip back to Berlin is via Copenhagen and Stockholm. The days of both business and pleasure with Moltke are Bonhoeffer's closest contact so far with the parallel Kreisau conspiracy. The debate with the young count, who is at that time against using force on Adolf Hitler, gives the actor portraying Bonhoeffer and the film as a whole a golden chance to justify the proposed guilt-ridden, long-argued, world-weighed, last-chance, no-alternative assassination of a destroying monster—and to distinguish that act from the lunatic, trigger-quick, self-advertisements of individuals who shoot celebrities for private reasons. The point is gravely serious, painfully delicate; dialogue at this point will have to be as brilliant as it is careful. Done right, it can be a major contribution to current national and international affairs.

Bonhoeffer had been preparing for a third wartime visit to Switzerland, when the Norwegian emergency took him north instead. Soon after his return, therefore, he is on his way again to Geneva. A day or two in Zurich first, then on to the ecumenical headquarters. Visser 't Hooft is not there, though, nor is Hans Schönfeld, a German minister in the ecumenical offices with whom he might have checked in, though Schönfeld had not always been entirely sympathetic with the Confessing Church or the claims Bonhoeffer had made for it in Geneva. The appearance of the young theologian is occasion for a staff party that evening, however, at which he overhears someone remarking that the Bishop of Chichester expected to be in Sweden at the end of May. Dietrich is suprised that his Swedish contacts in Berlin had not alerted him to that development. It would be a cruel disappointment not to see his dear friend if Bell got as close as the neutral soil in Stockholm. But even worse, it would be a wasted chance to give the Resistance story directly to a very vocal member of the British House of Lords, instead of spiriting it through again by all the back circuits so painfully developed. So Bonhoeffer changes his plans. The extra weeks in Switzerland are abruptly dropped. He returns to Zurich, checks up on the needs of the U-7 refugees there, and hastens to Berlin.

A week later he is on a late, stormy flight to Stockholm. Learning there that George Bell is at the church academy at Sigtuna, he proceeds north to the beautiful old town. And there, all unannounced, he simply walks in on his old friend. Astonishment and joy make a moment of jolting poignancy. Then Dietrich pours it all out. The whole story of the Resistance is told. By authorization of his Abwehr superiors he names names, so the Bishop can document the weight and significance of the conspiracy to his lords temporal: Beck, Canaris, Goerdeler, Leuschner, Hammerstein, Schacht (that seismograph, writes Bethge!), Kluge, Oster—all names of men the

English government will know. And in their name, Bonhoeffer repeats the hope that when the revolution is begun the Allies will give it a chance to succeed so a new government can bring a whole nation to the problems of restitution and renewal in that Europe over which the victorious Allies will have to preside. The Resistance is surer than ever that one word from the English indicating that they realize that there are forces in Germany working for the Allies' general ends will trigger the revolution in the only circle that now can get to Hitler.

Schönfeld arrives shortly, representing another circle of German conspirators, and is astonished to learn that Bell and Bonhoeffer are in private consultation. At a later general session Schönfeld is able to enlarge on the picture of the Resistance already given and to ask for the same sign from the English government. But it is just as well that Bonhoeffer had crashed the occasion. No one had to prove him to Bell, whereas the Bishop of Chichester remembered very well having once had to do battle himself for the Confessing Church against Pastor Schönfeld.

Anyway, the double insight is impressive. Warning the conspirators not to expect too much, Bell promises to get their request before Foreign Minister Anthony Eden (he does more than that, later; he goes to Eden—who has also had a memorandum from other conspirators via Visser 't Hooft—to Sir Stafford Cripps, to American Ambassador Winant; he speaks in the House of Lords; he writes for journals, always urging some kind of encouragement to any resistance there might be in Germany). The little group separates in Stockholm, having agreed on some code words for Bell to use when he cables results, probably through the Vatican. Bonhoeffer, taking warm leave of the distressed bishop, sends greetings by him to Sabine and Gerhard at Oxford and returns to Berlin.

A couple of June weeks meant to be spent resting in Klein-Krössin turn out instead to begin a whole new restlessness in Dietrich Bonhoeffer. For he is not the only visitor that summer in Ruth von Kleist's home. One of her granddaughters is there too, Maria von Wedemyer. The twelve-year-old, confirmation class reject, Maria von Wedemeyer. Only now the eighteen-year-old, beautiful, cultivated Maria von Wedemeyer.

First meetings, after six years, are full of humor, mock rue, with the aristocratic grandmother happily reassembling wraiths of her earlier wrath for the sunny occasion. . . . A table tennis game, undertaken *zum Erinnerung*, modulates somewhere in the second game as Dietrich finds his mind straying from the ball. By the third game, he is lost; he is even losing. Suddenly he is wild to begin those too-long-delayed confirmation classes. *This pagan must be taught a few things, but not here. As the Americans would say, out in God's cathedral of the pines, out under God's own vaulting sky; let's be "blue domers" as Dr. Coffin used to call them.*

The following days are given almost completely to the wandering "confirmation classes." The pious matriarch is full of phony disapproval. Almost no work is done on *Ethics.* The film will have to find swift ways to italicize this new line in the Bonhoeffer story. The loveliness will have very short life.

Before that month is over, Dietrich and Hans von Dohnanyi are on their way to Italy. In Venice they contact Wilhelm Schmidhuber, an anti-Nazi German businessman of occasional use to the Abwehr's Munich office. In Florence the sympathetic German consul puts them in touch with members of the Italian Resistance. In Rome they await word from Bell in London, get none, and return to Germany.

Bonhoeffer goes straight to Klein-Krössin and Maria. Hans returns to Switzerland in August, but Dietrich excuses himself to stay in Klein-Krössin. To work on the *Ethics*, of course. Except when he and Maria go to Berlin, separately, to do the city together. They may be there when Hans returns from Geneva with a copy of Bell's recent cable to Visser 't Hooft: There will be no

British encouragement for the Resistance at this time.

Early October, and Bonhoeffer is preparing for his most ambitious trip, to rally conspirators in Hungary, Bulgaria, Greece, Turkey, Croatia, and Italy. It would be a three-month adventure, perilous in the extreme, but fascinating. Just before his departure date, though, word arrives from Munich that Schmidhuber has been arrested by the Gestapo for passport and currency irregularities. His interrogation by the Gestapo is bound to reveal at very least his recent contact with von Dohnanyi and Bonhoeffer in Venice. The brothers-in-law know, furthermore, that as files are opened Schmidhuber's participation in the U-7 project will be noted—and, again, his connection with von Dohnanyi and Bonhoeffer. Beyond that, the amiable and not notably valiant Schmidhuber is unfortunately privy to the main facts about the whole Abwehr conspiracy.

The Gestapo thinks it may have found the crack into the Abwehr it has been looking for. As the Gestapo steps up its pressure it is encouraged by the Luftwaffe's Herman Göring, who for personal reasons very much wants a scandal in Admiral Canaris' department right now. And inside the Abwehr itself there are officers who are jealous of Hans and his swift rise in their service and of his obvious importance to Oster and

Canaris. Even if these junior colleagues will not at this time betray Dohnanyi, neither will they protect him.

It is not a time to leave beleagured relatives or a threatened operation. Or Maria. The long trip is put off. Instead, with every show of rectitude, the busy Abwehr agent Bonhoeffer hastens from Munich (to Klein-Krössin) to Freiburg to Magdeburg (to Klein-Krössin) to Berlin to Patzig.

Maria's mother lives in Patzig, and Maria's mother must now be dealt with. She knows it is not an uncontrollable affection for her own dear mother that takes Maria so often these days to Klein-Krössin. It is instead what begins to look like an uncontrollable affection for the brilliant, well-pedigreed, but increasingly mysterious, Dietrich Bonhoeffer. Grandmother von Kleist has been enthusiastic about him for years, but even she does not know what he is up to right now. So Bonhoeffer goes to Patzig—and cannot satisfy Frau von Wedemeyer. If he loves her very young daughter, can be really ask her to enter his quite mature life now, close-rimmed as it is with government prohibitions and interdictions? Of course it is going to get better. So why not wait until it does? Dietrich agrees to one year's complete separation from Maria.

That was November 24, 1942. By December he is in full rebellion. It was an impossible request and he had been a fool to agree. With Montgomery winning in the desert, the Americans safely ashore in Africa, Hitler's armies stopped at Stalingrad, the plotters' time is obviously near. Who could pledge a year to anything? Dietrich and Maria have ecstatic reunion—might it have been 12:01 A.M., January 1, 1943? That would have been a later year if not a year later.

On January 17, 1943, they are engaged. Only the parents are informed (not asked, this time), and Frau von Wedemeyer requests that they plan an extended engagement and make no public announcement for the time being. In early February young Maria meets the whole, overwhelming family. It takes all the Bonhoeffer parents' serenity and dignity to ease the happy excitement of the evening across ripping underground tensions.

At the end of January President Roosevelt and Prime Minister Churchill at Casablanca demanded "unconditional surrender." But in Russia the the German humiliation mounted. And at home the unpopular trial of some student "traitors" raised rumbles of public protest. Any moment now could be the moment.

On March 10 English news flashes carry word that His Majesty's government agrees with the Russians that not all Germans are necessarily Nazis. It is the first approximation of the cue the conspirators have needed. By March 13, Hans von Dohnanyi is delivering explosives to an airfield in Russia (Smolensk) where Schlabrendorff loads them onto Hitler's plane just before the Führer takes off on a return flight to his Prussian headquarters. The new English explosives do not detonate. On March 13 Dietrich Bonhoeffer is ordered to appear on March 22 for reconsideration of his draft exemption. General Oster has that order canceled.

On March 21 Major Rudolph von Gersdorff, with a bomb in each coat pocket, is chosen by the plotters to destroy Hitler, and himself if necessary, when standing near Hitler during a review scheduled for that day.

The whole Bonhoeffer clan is gathered at the Schleichers' that evening, to rehearse a cantata they will perform (all the children and the grandchildren except the Leibholzes) for Dr. Bonhoeffer's approaching seventy-fifth birthday. Dietrich is at the piano, Rudiger plays the violin, Klaus the cello, and Hans stands near them, singing with the chorus. The four. Hans' tension barely shows. His repeated looks at his watch are unobtrusive. If he checks on his car parked at the front door, he does so casually. And only Christine, sitting close by the telephone catches his glances at her. Ursula, concerned about her sister, who has had shaky moments since it became clear the Dohnanyis were being watched by the Gestapo, goes to stand beside her. But the telephone stays silent, Gersdorff never got his chance; Hitler changed his route.

It is an easy dissolve to Dr. Bonhoeffer's seventy-fifth birthday party one week later: same people, plus the elder Bonhoeffers. Sunday morning. Walcha's cantata *Lobe den Herren*, begun in rehearsal before, can be finishing now.

A congratulatory cablegram arrives from the Leibholzes, forwarded through Switzerland by Erwin Sutz. Klaus toasts his father, thanking him for what he has taught them of knowledge and truth. The whole happy scene goes suddenly surrealistic when a government agent appears at the door, only to read congratulations from the Führer, Adolph Hitler, on the birthday of the distinguished Dr. Karl Bonhoeffer and to award him in the name of the German people the prized Goethe Medal for Art and Science. (In a photograph of the occasion, Hitler's agent still smiles from the back row of the festively non-commital, conspiratorial family.)

The extraordinary day may end with a telephone call from Admiral Canaris to Hans and Dietrich, assuring them that all tracks are covered again, and that anything else that may come up about them can be easily handled. The men's relief is pale alongside that of Christine, the three of them grouped around the phone, apart from the others.

Dissolve to Dietrich again at the phone next morning, calling Christine so they can exult obliquely once more in their reassurance. While the call goes through he explains to Bethge that he had not realized until last night how nervous Christine has been. A man's voice, a stranger's, answers the telephone. Dietrich knows at once it is a Gestapo agent, and that the Dohnanyi's house is being searched. He excuses his wrong number and hangs up. He explains his hunch to Eberhard, suggests that they not disturb the napping parents and go at once next door to the Schleichers. There they explain to Ursula, then to Rüdiger; Ursula quickly prepares a big meal and the men stuff themselves on it. Dietrich and Eberhard return home hurriedly to check through the desk and drawers for incriminating papers, and to scatter a few innocent ones around. Turning over some old books, Dietrich shows Eberhard the inscriptions in two; each has been inherited from a great-grandfather's library, one Hase, one Tafel. *It is a coincidence*, says Bonhoeffer, *a century ago those two met, long before the families melded. They met in prison—they were resistors in their day.*

The young men return to the Schleichers, where they wait. About 4 P.M. Dr. Bonhoeffer comes slowly across the yard to say, *Two men want to talk to you upstairs in your room.* Bonhoeffer goes back with his father. They speak as they cross the lawn but we do not hear them. They stop at the front steps, face each other, yearning but not touching—it is the dignity that will see them all through—and Dietrich goes in alone.

Moments later he reappears between military Judge Manfred Roeder and Gestapo officer Franz Sonderegger. He is under arrest and on his way to the prison where Christine and Hans von Dohnanyi and Josef Müller are already locked up.

The Prisons

The climax of the film and the devastations at its end have everything going against them. Since the hanging of Dietrich Bonhoeffer was established in the opening scenes, there can be little suspense about his fate. And yet there is surging drama in the desperate fight to stay alive.

There is another kind of suspense, too, that can

be built on the violent alternations of hope. Especially as the story comes to its final sequences there is an almost daily shift between hopeful and desperate developments. No pendulum suffices for the image; this is no tick-tock back and forth. There is a huge clanging in the fateful alternation.

But the greatest shock left is in the size of the tragedy. Nothing in the opening scenes prepared anyone for the climactic engulfing of what should by now be a deeply respected, well-loved family. Not just Dietrich, but Klaus, Hans, and Rüdiger are destroyed; Christine and Eberhard imprisoned. It is this enlargement that permits the end of the film to mount beyond its shocking beginning in horror, remorse—and flooding compassion.

Now it is seen why it was suggested that so much time and attention be given, in slower early and middle passages, to the parents, brothers and sisters, friends. Extra footage given to them earlier will not be dawdling. On identities and identifications established there, the effect of the denouement now depends.

The same consideration bears on the other main complication. For what is *most* important about Dietrich Bonhoeffer—the development of ideas that have had revolutionary consequences not just in religion but in a whole generation's life style—reaches a climax in these same last scenes. Somehow, without slowing the pace, clogging the inevitability, or distorting the

rhythm of this last section, Bonhoeffer's intellectual perturbations must be signaled and the beginnings of his conceptual resolution set down.

Now all the earlier attention given to people
and places and things—the loving, long, quasi-
travelogue approach given to friends, family,
cities, landscapes, the arts—has its justification.
Because in the prison it is finally clear to Bonhoeffer that these are not preliminaries, happy
adjuncts to what is ultimately significant, but
bear their own huge meanings. In an autonomous
world, standing free at last from its metaphysical
frames, there need be no further theological
reservation about the exaltation of the earth and
its creatures.

At very least Bonhoeffer was finding his way
to a faith, a grip on the ultimate, which could in-
spire and fuel and orient action in this world (*all*
kinds of action) without becoming a prerequisite
to action in this world, without becoming a religion or a theology or an institution to be admired
and defended and decorated for itself.

At most, as radical commentators suggest, Bonhoeffer was on his way to deciding that the
ultimate is itself an extrapolation from the penultimate. It is hardly conceivable that the Bonhoeffer met in this film would have denied some
separate "being" to such ultimacy. But he very
well might not have spoken much about that,
except in the "secret discipline" he is so mysterious about. Publicly, the view elaborated here
would hazard that even the habitual pieties he

continued to set, halolike, around his most radical abstractions would probably have been lifted at last. And the language developed would have been that best calculated to insist on the basic, absolute importance of this life and this world. In this, Bonhoeffer has been followed by all significant theology written since his death.

In this interpretation (admittedly, wildly disputable) of Dietrich Bonhoeffer, from beginning to end he wanted to affirm men and their fascinating, confused, occasionally convulsed world, human culture, human relationships. Following Barth, and then going ahead of Barth, Bonhoeffer's instincts and ideas are organized formally in christological terms. But the special fascination in Bonhoeffer, now that Dr. Bethge's great biographical work is available, is the transparency of his development, the clear sight we have of the antecedent inclinations and experiences which are *subsequently* interpreted christologically. His strongly Christ-oriented interpretations and explanations have begun much for many; for Bonhoeffer they became, however, post scripts to his daily experience: diary summaries recorded in a theological shorthand learned earlier but used as time went on to report an increasingly novel vision of and mundane encounter with reality. His Christology (as long as he wrote that way), and with that his whole theology in all its phases, derives from his natively grateful, inquisitive, eager, worried, loving humanity. At the end he was apparently willing to waive the familiar curlicues in favor of the most direct possible affirmation of all that. He called what he was looking for a nonreligious interpretation of the gospel. It may as well have been a vernacular interpretation of the homely ultimacies immediately at hand.

STORY VII

The cut is savage: from the quiet, twilight woodsiness of the park around the big family houses, to the tiny, chilling, empty cell into which Dietrich Bonhoeffer is pushed in Tegel prison. The sound track fills in the screen's barren outline. The clanging of opened and closed doors, the banging on closed doors that will not open. The wretched sobbing of the man in the next cell. Far away, through many doors, the terrifying screams of a prisoner under torture, the incoherence of sudden relief, the renewed screaming screwed up higher, the babble of mad acquiescence.

Over all the sound, the surly, slovenly guard calling the goddamn no good to the door for his

dinner, a hunk of dry bread, which is not eaten—
but is not thrown away, either. Blankets are
heaved in next, and Dietrich drops them on the
cot. In this meticulous nation, the offense of their
odor must have been contrived, as will be the
fastidious pastor's endurance of them.

Only then is the legend noticed, scratched in
the wall by previous tenant: "What difference
will it make in one hundred years?" For Dietrich
there is neither comfort nor desolation in the
little cliché. He may talk back to the wall, *Probably none, no difference at all.* But if so, this is no
Stoic musing, seeking to defuse the present, to
lighten this present moment of its significance.
For Bonhoeffer the over-quoted question means
that since future meanings are discounted, the
present moment is all the more freighted. If the
only difference made is *now*, oh how important
that makes this Now, how full it must be made
to be.

His own effort to fill the treasured moment
takes two tacks. He occupies himself with getting
out, using every argument and stratagem against
the charges. And he lives as fully, humanely as
he can in the circumstances of the prison. Which
is not to say he knows no despair. On a scrap of
paper written soon after his arrest, desolation and
dignity struggle for utterance: *"Suicide, not because of a sense of guilt, but because basically I
am already dead. Full stop. The end."*

But, of course, it isn't the end. Not yet. And
meanwhile he will ponder the theological signifi-

cance of places and people and other "penultimates" without which life is basically over.

The military juridical activity begins slowly.
Hans, locked up in a prison for military officers,
is not confronted with Christine until eleven
days after their arrest (Christine is released several weeks later). Hans and Dietrich are brought
together two weeks after they are jailed. Though
the hearings for each were in fact separate and
covered several months, and the cast of legal
characters was assembled only gradually, for the
purposes of the film perhaps it will be best to
develop the charges and to introduce the judical
dramatis personae at the first confrontation.

Judge Roeder, hand in glove with the Gestapo,
is both prosecutor and judge; thus, he will bring
charges, document them, and frame the indictment he so desperately wants. He will hang Dietrich if he can but he *insists* on destroying Hans.
With Roeder, in the inquiry, are lawyers Lehmann and Sack, both high in the legal depart-
ments of the armed forces, and both protective
of the prisoners. One of Roeder's first motions,
for instance, is that the criminal Hans von
Dohnanyi be separated from his military commission. Lehmann overrules this for the announced reason that the alleged criminality is
exactly what has to be proved—and with the
private reason that decommissioning Hans now
would be to deliver him to the unscrupulous and

retributive Gestapo courts. As Roeder knew, too. Sack, whom the audience will recognize from earlier scenes when he worked with Oster's plotters (the audience is ahead of Roeder on this), does his part now by making sure the investigations will take a long time. He gets a private lawyer for Hans. Later he will get Dietrich permission to retain his own lawyer, too. He calls for careful deliberation.

In a hurried, whispered colloquy, while Lehmann preoccupies Roeder, Hans questions Sack's wisdom: *They know nothing, they have nothing, why don't we force this to an immediate judgment?* Dietrich is as urgent: *Let's just get out of here as fast as we can.* But Sack is careful: *You don't know what they have, I don't know what they have. Even if you got off here, the Gestapo would pick you up on its own charges. Meanwhile, we do know that something is going to happen to "someone." Let it happen. Then everything is over. Then whatever they have is to your* credit. *Play for time. It is on your side.*

The charges, insofar as Dietrich is concerned, are immediately forthcoming. First, his Abwehr association is scored as a transparent ruse to get around the Gestapo's prohibitions on his speaking and the Gestapo's requirement that he register his movements. Bonhoeffer's response, reiterated throughout the months as all his arguments will be, is that the Gestapo's interdictions were general and routine in the first place, not directed specifically at him, and that anyway his Abwehr

employment was bona fide. Any extra consideration it got for him was for the good of the job
and therefore for the nation. Besides, *he* did not
decide what freedoms he should reclaim; that was
his superiors' decision. He himself only followed
orders as any good citizen should.

This last is the incessantly repeated theme.
When questioned about a second charge having
to do with his activities in the U-7 incident he
lays full responsibility on Canaris and Dohnanyi.
Wherever actual plotting is approached, all parti-
cipants had long agreed to limit responsibility to
the leaders. The less evidence of any very extended apparatus they can give, the better. Even
the leaders will have an easier time if their mis-
takes can look private and impulsive. So Bonhoeffer insists, almost casually, that the only reason he even knows what Roeder is talking about
is that his friend Charlotte Friedenthal had left
Germany about that time. What time? Oh, long
ago: August, 1941, or so. The argument on date
is important because the later the little coup can
be placed, the more surely it can be considered a
sabotage of the government's own deportation of
Jews. So Bonhoeffer brazenly predates the episode. Sack points out that Admiral Canaris himself confirms all this, so the charge is dismissed.

A third charge has to do with all of Bonhoeffer's Abwehr trips out of the country. It provides
a field of investigation that could have been embarrassing, but it is very little ploughed. Evidence
is scant, and it is clear that Roeder cannot imagine

what baleful significance there could ever be in one preacher's talking to a lot of other preachers, whether they whispered or not.

The fourth charge is obviously the most agitating to Roeder, and it calls for the most outrageous and humiliating evasions from Bonhoeffer. This has to do with the alleged draft dodging of Confessing Church pastors—especially Bonhoeffer and Niesel—and the complicity of Dohnanyi who arranged so many of the questioned deferments. Bonhoeffer is all injured innocence. What could he possibly have wanted to avoid? Let anyone read his paragraphs in the *Cost of Discipleship* on Romans 13 with their endorsement of St. Paul's absolute command that Christians honor the state authorities; let anyone consider the heros in his own lineage who had died for Germany and the father and two brothers of his fiancée who are dead in this war; think of how he had come back in 1939 from a perfectly good job in New York; recall how he had tried to get appointment as a military chaplain—who can dare say he would ever try to avoid his patriotic duty? And as for Niesel and others, of course, they were deferred. Just before that happened he himself had had heartfelt talks with cabinet ministers of state, Gürtner and Kerrl, about how the schism in the German church must be healed and how the so-called Confessing Church pastors had to be given a chance to help bring spiritual strength to the embattled nation. Alas, good German Christians Gürtner and Kerrl have died since he, Bonhoeffer, had his patriotic concurrences with them, but those had been high, precious moments of spiritual unanimity. . . . And on and on and on.

The defense carries. Roeder is sure that it is all subterfuge, but he cannot prove it, so he must withdraw the charges of high treason against Bonhoeffer. They are dropped to a lesser charge of "sabotage against the armed forces," the cases of Bonhoeffer and Dohnanyi are set to be tried together, and the long wait begins for a trial that is never to come.

Bonhoeffer is in Tegel for eighteen months. The grimness of the first impressions is never relieved. But the little accommodations that make life bearable come from both sides. Except for very occasional evidence of anguish at the separation from everybody and everything he loves, Dietrich settles into a regime of study, reflection, and writing that keeps him steady between interrogations and alarms. His high academic and military connections do him no harm among his goalers when those ties become known.

And he is his impressive self, even in the tense and artificial society of jail. Some guards maintain their surly contempt throughout, but most capitulate to the Bonhoeffer charm and his honest interest in them and their families and their thinking. They actually bargain among themselves for the chance to work on Bonhoeffer's floor. Dur-

ing exercise periods some ask to be photographed
with him (there one stands in the snapshot we
have still: tall, proud, uniformed guard at the end
of a short line of well-dressed young men, Dietrich pleasant, dignified, elegant, a little aloof in
the middle, neighbors on each side leaning in on
him, ever so slightly). They smuggle letters in
and out of the prison for him, so Bethge gets un-
censored accounts of his friend's life and thinking
to supplement the careful reports sent the family
in the weekly authorized mail. One guard offers
to share his own ample rations with Bonhoeffer's
parents. One asks for prayer. One apologizes as
he locks Bonhoeffer in for the night.

A certain community develops among the
prisoners, too. Ordinarily there would have been
little time for contact among them in Tegel. But
then, as Allied air attacks on German cities mount
there are frequent air-raid drills and even the first
air raids, in all of which Bonhoeffer roams the
prison as an ambulance man. More and more frequently the friendly guards invite Dietrich down
to the little infirmary, too, where he meets other
prisoners, hears foreign newscasts on the short
wave, hears music: Beethoven's "Missa Solemnis,"
Reger, Palestrina (remembering the long ago
vespers in the Trinitá del Monte), Pfitzner
(whom even the sound-starved Dietrich found
very so-so).

Predictably, he gets involved in some of his
fellow prisoners' lives. He rallies his father and

his own lawyer to the defense of an English officer and an Italian partisan who are in danger of execution, and both are saved. He cuts dead one prisoner, on his way to being a friend, until he drops an anti-Semitic slur. He writes his relative, General Paul von Hase (met several times earlier in the film, always in happy occasion), who is military commandant of all Berlin prisons, asking for attention to unnecessary privations and inefficiencies at Tegel.

The interrogations continue into August. On September 25, 1943, Bonhoeffer's official indictment is handed down. Hope mounts for an early consideration of the case. In October a date is actually set for the Bonhoeffer–Dohnanyi trial: December 17, 1943. Bonhoeffer is so elated he writes Maria about the plans he is making for their wedding.

But there is no trial. On November 23, 1943, there is an air raid on Berlin, during which an incendiary bomb penetrates Hans' cell. He is not killed, but suffers a crippling brain embolism. Sack, terribly anxious, induces Lehmann to order Dohnanyi's removal to the famous Berlin hospital, Charité, where the celebrated Dr. Sauerbruch can care for the son-in-law of his celebrated colleague, Dr. Bonhoeffer. The transfer is made, and Judge Roeder, arriving late, immediately tries to return the gravely ill man to his shattered prison. Neither law nor military might impresses Dr.

Sauerbruch in the least. With that authority un-
matched in the world, the private will of the
prima donna physican, he cuts Roeder dead and
announces that Hans von Dohnanyi will stay
where he is. Roeder, bested on that front, bossily
orders no visitors for his prisoner; Sauerbruch
makes it clear that he will decide what is good
for his patient.

And so they come: family, friends, the new
conspirators, taking back streets, stealing in from
the darkness so they will not give undue advance
notice to Roeder's guards. At first urgently, then
frantically, Hans begs his colleagues to see to the
destruction of his secret "chronicles," that careful, voluminous documentation of Nazi infamy.
He knows that if they are ever found, he and
many others are surely doomed. But always the
word comes back: General Beck will not hear of
the fearful archive's destruction. Finally these
documents and their dates and their editor's stature may be the only witness to the early response
of the resistance to Hitler's crimes. Without the
chronicles the conspirators may seem disgruntled
officers tardily turning on a losing superior. With
the chronicles, those who care may know that
some human beings fought back early in their
nation's hell. So Hans begs, but Beck holds.

The new conspirators who visit the hospital
include family. A group is forming around young
Count von Stauffenberg, who has occasional access to the Führer. Klaus, Rüdiger, Eberhard are

involved. The plotting is aggressive: junior officers Baron Axel von dem Bussche and the 20
year old Ewald von Kleist have their bombs hidden in a pile of new uniforms they are to deliver
to Hitler, but the dictator's eerie luck holds
again: The uniforms are lost in a fire. So new
plans have to be made.

Meanwhile, because of Hans' incapacitation,
the first trial date for him and Dietrich goes by.
Days later Roeder sends an ambulance for the
patient who is apparently well enough to hold
nocturnal court. Dr. Sauerbruch will not hear of
his removal. It could be that after this rebuff
Roeder secretly commissions Gestapo man Sonderegger to dig even harder for anything that
might further incriminate Dohnanyi and Bonhoeffer. And then Roeder talks superior authority
into sending Professor de Crinis (Dr. Bonhoeffer's
successor in the psychiatry chair at the university) for an independent opinion on Hans'
condition.

Successors are not tender of predecessors' sen-
sitivities. Professor de Crinis finds Hans ready to
travel. In January, 1944, while Dr. Sauerbruch is
away from the Charité, Roeder transports Dohnanyi to the prison hospital, Buch. And sets a
February date for the trial.

February 4, 1944, is Dietrich's thirty-eighth
birthday. Two guards somewhat sheepishly bring

him flowers for the occasion. The day goes on as cheerily as possible. Then he is called down to the visiting room to receive a package from home. Maria is the courier! Contact is forbidden; affection strains across space. But words are free. And such words: Renate and Eberhard Bethge have had a baby, a son, to be called Dietrich, born the day before the great-uncle's (the great-uncle shudders) birthday. Alone again in his room, Bonhoeffer checks the books included in his birthday package. On one, his name inside the cover is underlined. That means it contains a coded message. Starting at the back, he works forward through the book, seeking one lightly marked letter on every tenth page. Slowly the message emgerges: Canaris is fired, betrayed by an Abwehr agent in Turkey.

That afternoon a sudden visit by the tense Dr. Sack discloses the rest. Canaris' whole Abwehr outfit has been disbanded and its work handed over to the Gestapo. So the Bonhoeffer and Dohnanyi case is now in the hands of those from whom they had fought to keep it. Sack is more than ever determined to hold things up. The Gestapo's first moves could have been worse. For instance, Roeder has been replaced. Hans' report to friends, while in the Charité, that Roeder had called one group of the Abwehr "shirkers," had brought the group's superior officer to see Hans. On hearing confirmation of the report the general proceeded directly to the judge's office and publicly boxed Roeder's ears! Roeder was shortly thereafter kicked upstairs to Bulgaria. The new judge appointed to the case has already allowed Christine to visit Hans again; Hans' civilian lawyer is consulting regularly; Müller's case has been completely separated from Bonhoeffer's and Dohnanyi's, and Müller is found not guilty.

So time may do it all. But how to get time? Sack wretchedly reports Dohnanyi's solution. He has asked and received from Christine a culture of scarlet fever and diphtheria. He chewed it down immediately, and now lies, paralyzed, in an isolation ward in a Potsdam sanatorium. The new judge, after interviewing Hans through a window, has decided to postpone the whole case until after the war, with Dohnanyi remaining in the sanatorium.

Dietrich is deeply distressed by the long sound of "after the war." He would have been even more distressed if his marked books had not hinted at a July action that could end it all soon. And now some visitors add to the ebullience that never flags for long.

First, Eberhard, locked in with him alone for an hour by a sympathetic guard. Awkward first moments, then tongues are hung in the middle, and the fast talk is on. Family talk from Eberhard, family questions from Dietrich. Then questions from Eberhard about the extraordinary ideas Dietrich has been suggesting in his recent letters: about a world come of age, a world rightly accepting its responsibility and declaring its disinterest in metaphysics and its independence of mother church, a free, autonomous secularized world that should be *hailed* rather than deplored by the Christian! Dietrich's talk is all excited tentativity: *I do not know where the new line is going to take me, but I am on my way. I cannot get interested anymore in celebrating a mighty God who sits way out on the edge of the universe, the Great Answer Man in the Sky, the solution to doleful problems that only preachers ask, claiming that nobody else can solve them— yet. I am through with theologies that throw you solid lead pellets of doctrine that have to be swallowed whole before anything else can happen* (and he mentions Barth in this category). *My old distaste for "religion" is now monumental. I am not sorry there is no church to go to here, I go long periods without reading the Bible, when men moan, "O God, O God," under bombardment, I do not pray or say pious things to them, but look at my watch and say, "Hang on, friend, it will be over in another nine minutes." I am trying for a faith that is found in, and that puts me in, the middle of life and the world, loving them both, and willing with Christ to suffer what is necessary with and for them.*

A few days later there is a visit from General Paul von Hase, Berlin commandant and Mrs. Bonhoeffer's cousin. Tegel is agog: the high commander, and to visit a *prisoner*. Dietrich joins the general in the finest office in the prison. Von Hase has brought food and wine; he stays five hours with his younger relative. He is apologetic, *I wish there were something I could do for you. . . .* Bonhoeffer is the host wherever he is, *And I you. . . .* The general tries to explain, *You know the danger to the whole family if I should show any . . .* Dietrich interrupts, *I know, I know; that is how far we have come* [a guard, going through, looks his disapproval and Dietrich elides smoothly] *from the evening games in your father's garden. But just your being here is much. . . .* The general: *It is little, it is late, it is the least I can do.* Dietrich picks him up: *And the most maybe; sometimes it is the most any of us can do, just be there, with the other, for the other. I sometimes think that is what it is all about, being for others; whatever else you say about Jesus Christ, he was always the man for others.*

Alternatively, this might be the place to suggest Bonhoeffer's germinal connection with what has since been called "contextual" or "situational" ethics. The clearest illustration would come from his treatment of "truth." By the time of his arrest, he had written very clearly on this, and surely it would be a natural subject for the relatives' discussion. Both are men of unimpeachable probity; and both are plotters, living lies. The general, whole-heartedly in the conspiracy, might well wonder what the theologian makes of truth in as twisted a situation as theirs. Which gives Bonhoeffer his chance to say what he had already worked out for his *Ethics*: the truth has to do with more than verbal veracity, it has to do with the reality and the quality of human relationships; the truth is that which serves and preserves honesty between people. Precisely what "telling the truth" will mean in any situation depends not just upon moral character but upon sensitivity to, reflection on, and the readiness to make a new decision about the particular human threats and possibilities in the specific situation in question. "An individual utterance is always part of a total reality which seeks expression in this utterance. If my utterance is to be truthful it must in each case be different according to whom I am addressing, who is questioning me, and what I am speaking about. The truthful word is not in itself constant; it is as much alive as life itself."

But having said something like that (in the vernacular, of course) Bonhoeffer would also want to protest any effort to fit the conspiracy or the conspirators into any general rule, however comprehensive. He had covered that too in his *Ethics*: "In the course of historical life there comes a point where the exact observance of the formal law of a state . . . suddenly finds itself in violent conflict with the ineluctable necessities of the lives of men; at this point responsible and pertinent action leaves behind it the domain of principle and convention, the domain of the normal and regular, and is confronted by the extraordinary situation of ultimate necessities, a situation which no law can enforce."

Dietrich Bonhoeffer knows well why he does what he does, why he is where he is. His whole valiant, supple ethics is framed in prayer for and confidence of forgiveness for what may go wrong in such chancy morality. Without such confidence, the teaching is intolerable. With such confidence no other teaching is tenable.

Even so, back in his own cell, he agonizes over what the emergency complexities will do to ensuing simplicities. He writes to Eberhard: ". . . we have learned the arts of equivocation and pretence; experience has made us suspicious of others and kept us from being truthful and open; intolerable conflicts have worn us down and even made us cynical. Are we still of any use? What we shall need is not geniuses, or cynics, or misanthropes, or clever tacticians, but plain, honest, straightforward men. Will our inward power of resistance be strong enough, and our honesty with ourselves remorseless enough for us to find our way back to simplicity and straightforwardness?" And that question is still another controlling theme big and thick enough all by itself for an important dramatic shaping of Bonhoeffer's life and thought.

And then, early in June, Maria. The same friendly guard locks them in alone, too, and the scene should probably fade as he walks away from the door. If it is continued, later, the excited whispering should all be about the new attempt on Hitler's life now set for mid-July. Everything has to be said by indirection, but it is clear that this is to be the major stroke by the Stauffenberg circle, which includes Klaus, Rüdiger, Eberhard. Leave-taking is therefore relatively lighthearted. Lasting reunion is in sight.

Count von Stauffenberg's briefcase was moved behind a table leg at the July 20 staff meeting so Adolf Hitler was not killed by the explosion— which, however, now uncovered layers of well-buried conspiracy.

At 7:30 A.M. the next day the telephone rings at the Bonhoeffers', and a familiar voice asks for Hans von Dohnanyi. The call is transferred to Christine, and so she hears from Gestapo man Sonderegger (who had arrested Christine, Hans, and Dietrich in the first place) that he is at last in charge of the Dohnanyi–Bonhoeffer case. He explains that he will move Hans shortly from his "permanent" Potsdam asylum to the concentration camp at Sachsenhausen. The adjourned case is wide open again. The Stauffenberg ring has been blown, and the Führer is ravening for the life of everybody even remotely connected. While these remote connections are being traced to Dohnanyi and Bonhoeffer, Mrs. Dohnanyi will be advised not even try to visit her husband.

At Tegel, Dietrich is sure his life is over. Still

privy to the clinic radio, he documents the collapse of hope. The suicide of Oster is rumored; Canaris is arrested; immediate conspirators are getting summary judgments and execution. General Paul von Hase has been hanged. Dietrich writes to Maria begging her now to avoid Berlin.

At the Bonhoeffer home, two months later, it is clear that Maria is more permanently installed than ever. To avoid government draft she has been designated Dr. Bonhoeffer's assistant. In laboratory smock now, she admits prison guard Knobloch to the room where Ursula, Rüdiger, and Renate Schleicher wait with Mother Bonhoeffer to continue the planning that is obviously already well advanced. The scheme is for Dietrich to flee the prison. In workingman's clothes smuggled in by his relatives, he will leave Tegel with Knobloch; both will disappear into Berlin and then hide out till the end.

Even as the plotters bend low to their whispers, the indefatigible Sonderegger is discovering a large file of Hans' Chronicles, hidden in an inconspicuous part of a remote air-raid shelter (September 22, 1944). Taken at once to Hitler, the files change his mind: The executions are suspended. Everyone mentioned in the files is to be kept alive until every morsel of extractable evidence is torn from him. Hope may flare again, but not much.

Two days later, Ursula, Rüdiger, and Renate take the rough clothes to Knobloch, to be hidden in his garden tool shed. The escape is one week away.

Six creeping, endless days later, Klaus, returning home in the evening, sees the fateful long black Mercedes of the SS parked at his door. He hurries to the Schleichers, to find pandemonium. Mrs. von Hase, widow of the general, just released from jail and branded by her husband's shame, has been turned away by every friend or relative to whom she turned for shelter. Frantic, she has come at last to the Schleichers who receive her and try to still the hysterics—and brace themselves for the new official attention now inevitably focused on an already nervous household. Then Klaus adds his report. In the midst of all this, Knobloch arrives with requests from Dietrich for certain papers and passes that will be necessary in his flight. The good messenger is told Klaus' news, and returns hastily to Tegel. All that night the tormented Klaus and rock-solid Ursula (Emmi and the children are safely in the country) discuss the possible choices: flight, suicide, surrender.

Next morning (October 1, 1944), Klaus is arrested. Sometime the following day Knobloch brings back the worker's clothes: Dietrich will not attempt escape. The family needs no more pressure or attention. Two days later, Rüdiger, Schleicher and Eberhard Bethge are arrested. Next day, Sonderegger tells Hans it is all over. More papers have been found; the Gestapo has what it wants. On October 8, Dietrich Bonhoeffer is moved from Tegel to the Gestapo prison on Prinz Albrechtstrasse.

The film can show reunions, surprising ones, surprisingly staged. They happen in the showers where the prisoners meet every morning, buck naked under the icy spray. The scene should be a striking composition of the ludicrously bizarre and the mordantly fateful. These are dead men, but they gasp in the cold water, make arch introductions, whisper frantically beneath the clamor. They are all there: Canaris, Oster, Sack, Goerdeler, Schlabrendorff, Müller. And Bonhoeffer.

Hans is still in Sachsenhausen. Klaus, Rüdiger, and Eberhard are in the Lehrterstrasse prison, sequestered with the group charged most specifically with the July 20 plot. Their trial will come first; the inquiry into their complicity is conducted by a separate commission under Judge Roland Freisler (later called "Raving Roland" by Allied jurists studying Nazi records) and is based on independent documentation. Prosecution of the Abwehr group with which Dietrich and Hans are involved is still being pressed by Sonderegger on the strength of the so-called "Zossen papers," which are a part of Hans' "Chronicle of Nazi Scandals" and now finally betrayed by a colleague—whom the judicious Hans never permitted Christine to name, even after the Gestapo told them who the traitor was.

So the grotesquerie of the shower scene degenerates into the nightmare of interrogation. Klaus is tortured. Eberhard is confronted with a claimed confession signed by Dietrich—but Eberhard recognizes the sentences above the signature, when the document is flashed at him, as coming from a much earlier technical manuscript of Bonhoeffer's, and he is not trapped. Over in Prinz Albrechtstrasse Dietrich is threatened again and again with what will be done to his parents, Maria, his sisters, if he does not talk. He admits, *insists*, his Christian aversion to National Socialism and its totalitarian demands, but nothing else. He no doubt is permitted to hear the wild screaming of men under torture around him. (Could Maria hear this too, outside? She does get as far as the prison office, where Sonderegger is pleased to tell her she cannot see Dietrich. Then she is off to Pätzig, to help her mother move young relatives west, before the advancing Russians.) In Sachsenhausen, the invalid Hans on his litter is savaged and brutalized by interrogators who shout, *You are only alive because Der Führer says you must not die until you tell him exactly how July 20 could have come about.*

In between, at the Gestapo prison, the Abwehr men share their cigars as they get them, meet for their macabre badinage at the chilly morning rendezvous, and comment on the strange diffidence of some of their interrogators, a vague uneasiness that alternates with cruel bluster, compounding the tension. *They know they've lost,*

some say. *They don't want us to remember them
as all bad.* Someone quotes Hans; *they are heaving
their anchors into the future.*

February, 1945 and the chill is in more than
the showers. The Gestapo prison heating system
breaks down and bitter cold settles into the cells.
Unknown to Dietrich, Hans is brought to the
freezing prison on the first of the month. On
February 3, their section of Berlin crumples under
ferocious air attack by the Allies. Pandemonium
in the stricken prison. All surviving testimony is
that Dietrich Bonhoeffer was always larger than
life in such calamity. Moving down the aisle of
locked-in prisoners clamoring to be taken to the
bomb shelters, he invokes no religious phrases, but
with steady good sense reinforces common life
in the midst of death. So, perhaps, to a jibbering
fifteen-year-old after a close explosion: *As we
boys used to say in a thunderstorm, "we heard
that one, so it didn't get us, eh Curt?"* Or to a
musical comrade, speechless after a particularly
thunderous explosion: *A little heavy on the bass,
that one,* nicht wahr, *Franz?* (But by himself, he
is not so sure. In his letters and in his most poign-
ant poem, "Who Am I?" he wonders about
where to locate him*self*, between the calm and
the courage he is credited with, and the private
terror he must confess.)

In the bomb shelter there is the usual quiet
stirring of some of the guards who maneuver to
stand near the serene preacher who does not talk
like a preacher. When the raid is over, as if to

make up for the momentary weakness, the guards are all brisk celerity: *Move along, move along, back to your cells.* But not all cells are there, after this attack, so there is confusion in the hallways. Dietrich finds himself beside an open door, looking down into Hans' drawn, feverish face. For a moment he is not sure—they have not seen each other for a year and a half, and Hans has been dangerously ill most of that time. Then Hans recognizes Dietrich, raises his hand slightly, and Dietrich dares dart into the room. He is wrenched with remorse at sight of the frail wreck on whom he has been dutifully placing all responsibility for anything the government questioned. Dietrich kneels beside the cot, but Hans motions him not to come too close. *I am sick again, Christine smuggled me another diphtheria strain. It is our only hope now, Dietrich—time. We must be here when the end comes. Someone must make it end, and we must still be here. Do you hear anything about anyone planning?* Dietrich is overwhelmed by Hans' deterioration. *Perhaps; but Hans, I cannot put it all on you anymore. I know we agreed, but now I must take my share.* Hans blazes. *Of course you will go on as before. Don't* dare *change a word.* Everything *depends on that; one change of any kind now, and all previous testimony will look false. They'd have us all.* And then, falling back, *Dietrich, the Gestapo knows everything about me, they found my "chronicle." Now they want more;* don't *give them anything else to ask me about . . .*

Dietrich slips into the line of prisoners still filing past the open door.

Other Bonhoeffers had other experience in the same air raid (the separate events are too full of motion and essential dialogue to share a split screen, perhaps, but their simultaneity will be suggested by the flickering, fiery reminders of the raid in all the seriatum scenes).

On the afternoon of February 2, 1945, Judge Freisler had pronounced the death sentence on Klaus and Rüdiger. That evening they passed Eberhard's cell on their way to Death Row in the Lehrterstrasse prison. Early the next morning, February 3, Ursula with her daughter Dorothee and Rüdiger's brother, Dr. Rolf Schleicher, head for the government center to seek audience with the minister of justice. They will appeal the sentences. Then the air raid holds them in the subway station below the government center for two hours. Just before the all clear, a desperate call for a doctor comes down the steps. Rolf hurries to respond, and is taken straight to the courthouse they had been trying to get to. The distinguished victim has been hit by a bomb fragment and is dead. In a courthouse of course a death certificate is immediately forthcoming, and Dr. Schleicher is asked to sign it as attending physician. Only then does Rolf realize that it is Judge Freisler stretched out before him, his brother's prosecutor, judge, and hangman. The physician refuses to sign the certificate until he has seen the minister of justice. That august worthy is nonplussed by this extraordinary intrusion, but hears Rolf out, and grants a delay of execution to Rüdiger and Klaus with a reevaluation of the indictment after a plea for mercy is entered. With satisfaction, Dr. Schleicher signs the death certificate.

Meanwhile, Ursula and Dorothee have reached the untouched Lehrterstrasse prison, and discovered that Rüdiger and Klaus are unharmed.

At the same time all this is going on, Dr. and Mrs. Bonhoeffer and Klaus' wife Emmi are trying to deliver a birthday package to Dietrich at Prinz Albrechtstrasse. Dr. Bonhoeffer is determined to see his youngest son. But this little party too is pinned down in the subway by the air raid. When the all clear comes, there is no way forward. Rubble chokes all avenues, and word comes back that the Gestapo prison itself has been hit. Filthy, exhausted, they fight their way home, whence Emmi at once sets out to visit her husband, Klaus, at the Lehrterstrasse jail.

On Dietrich's birthday, February 4, the family gets news that nobody in the Gestapo prison was hurt. On February 7 they send a parcel in to him, which includes a volume of Plutarch. On February 14, which is the next permissible parcel day, they deliver a package again, only to be told that Dietrich Bonhoeffer was sent out of Berlin on February 7.

Two trucks came at noon that day. Twenty prisoners were assembled in the prison yard and divided between the trucks, one headed for Flossenbürg, the other for Buchenwald. Müller and Bonhoeffer were handcuffed, and Dietrich protested the gratuitous indignity. Müller murmured, *Let us go to the gallows like Christians.*

It was late night when Bonhoeffer and his group arrived at the concentration camp in Buchenwald, with some relief at discovery of their destination. Fearful enough rumors circulate about Buchenwald, but they are not as baleful as those about Flossenbürg.

The new prisoners have been taken directly to the cells established for "the condemned elite." The cells are not elegant. Built in the basement of houses outside the camp, the little rooms are damp, cold, and utterly without daylight. When air raids are signaled, the guards simply lock the prisoners in and leave; it is not comforting to those thus enclosed to know that large munitions stores are stacked in the same basement.

But contact between the prisoners is much more generous here, perforce. Since the cells are buried outside the camp fences, there is no possibility of outdoor exercise. Instead, the prisoners are allowed to pace the three long halls that divide the dim rooms. Then, two weeks after the Prinz Albrechtstrasse contingent arrives, a new lot of distinguished prisoners clatters down the steps. General von Rabenau, until recently the chief archivist for the military forces, is moved in as

Bonhoeffer's cellmate. The general is an urbane, scholarly man, working at his memoirs. During the corridor strolls, he introduces Dietrich to other members of the group with whom he arrived. Most interesting of these, perhaps, is Vassily Kokorin, Russian air force officer, and the youthful nephew of Russian Foreign Secretary Molotov. In another of those hospitable showerrooms, Bonhoeffer also meets the young English pilot, Payne Best, who contributes chessmen and a board to the full life.

The general turns out to be an interesting companion. Older than most of the others, between his dismissal from the service and his arrest he had gone back to the university to work for a theological degree. He delights in long arguments with his academically distinguished younger cellmate. Being one generation earlier than Bonhoeffer in his basic orientation, Rabenau probably speaks more of "principles." That is a sure goad to Bonhoeffer; he never would hear of principles. They too easily take the place of God. Even He is made to conform to them, when in fact "principles are only tools in God's hand, soon to be thrown away as unserviceable." And look what "principles" do to men: Pursuing "principles" they either concentrate on the private purity of their own pursuit, or they remorselessly press their precious iron "principles" down on all society—and in neither case have they paid attention to what ethics is really about, the present needs of living men. The more successful the principle pusher is, the bigger his failure. ". . . it is a failure because here no true encounter has taken place at all with life, with man; it is rather that something alien, false, imaginary and at the same time completely tyrannical has been superimposed on man without really and essentially affecting him, changing him and forcing him to a decision. Ideologies vent their fury on man and then leave him as a bad dream leaves a waking dreamer. The memory of them is bitter. They have not made the man stronger or more mature; they have only made him poorer and more mistrustful."

The dialogue must be written in the vernacular, of course. But the above quotes from Bonhoeffer's *Ethics* state the conclusions to which he has come, the convictions that must somehow be stated before the death. The Christ he was thinking about now was less than ever a proclaimer of principles, rules, commandments that were good once, are good, and will always be good. "Christ teaches no abstract ethics such as must at all costs be put into practice. Christ was not essentially a teacher and a legislator, but a man, a real man like ourselves. And it is not therefore His will that we should at all times be the adherents, exponents, and advocates of a definite doctrine, but that we should be men, real men before God. Christ did not, like a moralist, love a theory of good, but He loved the real man. He was not, like a philosopher, interested in the 'universally valid,' but rather in that which is of help to the real and concrete human being. What worried Him was not, like Kant, whether 'the maxim of an action can become a principle of general legislation,' but whether my action is at this moment helping my neighbor to become a man before God. For indeed it is not written that God became an idea, a principle, a program, a universally valid proposition or a law, but that God became *man*."

The corridor friendship with Kokorin developed quickly, too. The personable and sensitive Russian seems to have epitomized for Bonhoeffer both that new generation that would take quite for granted a responsible world competent to its own affairs *and* that group of contemporaries with whom he had worked in the conspiracy who shared few of his theological preconceptions but who were keener about the world and its real values than were many of the churchmen with whom he had worked earlier. Kokorin was at home in the world come of age, a Communist who knew little of God but who defended life, truth, justice, goodness, decency—man. And Bonhoeffer was at home with him.

The Russian's questions were simpler than the general's. They were, in fact, the same that Dietrich's church friends had often asked before. Only with them they were thrown out as challenges, often with condemnation implicit. With Kokorin, though, they were honest, interested inquiry. *As a Christian pastor, Dietrich, how do you explain your involvement in this political conspiracy?* Bonhoeffer has often before used the image: *If I were walking down the Kurfursten-damm and saw a racing car striking some pedestrians and imperiling more, I would not consider I had done my whole Christian duty if I at once began to comfort the victims. It would be as much my responsibility as anyone's to stop that car. The Christian is more than a nurse's aid and the minister is more than a chaplain. We do what we can in whatever field to save life and serve man . . . and first things first.*

Which brings up the second fundamental question again: *But even so, restraining the automobile is one thing; surely, for a Christian, killing the driver is another?* Bonhoeffer refuses to let the image be so forced. He shifts similes: *In my Barcelona days we were often at the bullring. There I studied the stupidity of the great beast. Always he attacked the cape, the aggravating scarlet. He never seemed to realize that there was someone at the center of the maddening phenomenon, a man who shook out the infuriating silk; someone central, not something peripheral, that must be put away if the torment was ever to stop.*

In exactly these days, by train and bus and foot, Maria is scouring Germany between Berlin and Nuremberg for Dietrich. She lugs a suitcase full of warm clothes for him. She gets to the outer enclosures of both Flossenbürg and Buchenwald, undoubtedly walks over the cells in which Dietrich is buried, but is turned away and drags her way back to Berlin.

There, the Bonhoeffer women make their incessant trips to the prisons where their men wait. Every scrap of anything good they can get goes straight to the prisoners. Ursula, especially, loses weight drastically. Rüdiger, knowing at whose expense the extra offerings must be, sends some back to his wife.

Even without music, Easter dawn (April 1, 1945) at Buchenwald has the sound of resurrection. The Americans' great guns can be heard from the Werra River. Hope flashes down the dim corridors. Surely now there will be neither time nor place for courts or trials? The men are quiet; no one wants to miss a note or beat of the thunderous Easter anthem.

Then comes the ominous order: Prepare for departure. The distinguished prisoners will leave the camp as soon as transportation is available. If it is not shortly forthcoming, they will walk. That addendum is most troubling. It is by now standard for judicial embarrassments to be lined up in the woods and shot before an advancing enemy breaks through.

For two days there is tearing contest between enemy cannon and native terror. On April 3, late in the evening, transport arrives from Berlin. Somewhere in that shattered city and crumbling government, forms are still being filled out, and officials are keeping schedules, and equipment is being dispatched. So the wood-burning truck finally smokes into Buchenwald. The back of the closed truck is full of wood, of course: That is what it runs on. Jammed into space that might have held eight, sixteen "prominents" wrap themselves around logs and each other. The truck gropes along the road at twenty miles an hour. Every hour the carburetor has to be cleaned and the fire box filled. That means fresh air, at least, and another bit of expansion space for every log lifted out. Bonhoeffer finds some tobacco in his pocket, when he can finally get to it, and contributes it "to the common good," as the Englishman Best says.

They all need whatever comfort there is in it. All they know is that they are driving south all night. Flossenbürg is south, and Flossenbürg is the worst. At dawn they stop for breakfast (military rations, a novelty) in the forest. Then on to the south. At Weiden, where they should turn east if they are going to Flossenbürg, there is indistinct consultation in the truck's cab. Then the truck stops. A policeman's voice is heard at some unseen crossroad: *Go on, we can't take you—too full.* Relief is a strange radiance in the dark truck, which chugs on south again.

Then, the familiar unease. Police motorcycles are heard in the distance behind them, then closer, then throttling down by the back doors of the truck. They are flung open, Müller and Liedig are told to bring their gear and jump out; they will be returning to Flossenbürg. As the sunshine pours through the open doors, Bonhoeffer almost reflexively shrinks back out of the identifying light. Gehre, though, leaps out to join Müller. They have been cellmates at Buchenwald; he wants to stay with his friend.

After that, the guards loosen up. Flossenbürg is behind them, and there should be no more retrievals—not with benzin as scarce as it is. At a farmhouse the prisoners are allowed to splash and scrub around the water pump. The farmer's wife brings them milk and bread. By sunset the clumsy vehicle is in Regensburg. No place to go but the city jail, and the warden is not glad to see them: *More aristocrats! It is five to a cell here*. The jail kitchen is closed, but the ebullient new tenants, freer for every kilometer put between themselves and Flossenbürg, shout and clatter until an apprehensive guard brings them soup and bread.

Next morning, when cell doors are open so prisoners can go to the wash rooms the corridors turn into boulevards. It is a reunion. The families of conspiratorial colleagues are all jailed here: Goerdelers, Stauffenbergs, Halders, Hammersteins, Hassells, wives and children. The guards are helpless to reorganize the prisoners as the tearful, laughing, talkative meetings go on. Even when the men are back in their cells, Bonhoeffer talks on and on, through the crack in a sliding door, with Frau Goerdeler. He had spoken to her husband as he went to his execution. An air raid interrupts the happy buzz, but after Berlin the noise is nothing, so talk goes on in the basement. By the time they are all lying down again in their cells, Dietrich is sure the worst of everything is over.

But late that rainy night the stinking old truck is heard beneath the jail windows, and shortly the Buchenwald contingent is back in its shallow cavern. But they do not get far this time. After a few miles a new clatter develops, the mechanism dies, and they stop beside the dark Chaussee, burned out vehicles all around, machine guns at the alert, and the cold rain pounding on the roof. At dawn the prisoners are released to stretch and wander briefly, then back into the truck. It is noon before a replacement bus arrives with ten new heavily armed SS guards inside. The bus is faster, the drive along the Danube somehow heartening. When the driver stops for repartee with some hitchhiking girls, he explains his dubious entourage as a movie company off to make a war film. The prisoners do their ironic best to justify their casting. The bus stops at a farmhouse for eggs—for the guards.

By afternoon they are in Schönberg, in a great, shining second-floor schoolroom with real beds. The family survivors from the Regensburg jail are already here, in their own rooms, so again the corridor greetings. Bonhoeffer flings open a big window, strips off his shirt, and for the first time in months begins to put color back on his still athletic body. Sitting in the sun, he and Kokorin go on with the Russian lessons begun some time before. Villagers bring in food; the men create the effect of permanence by writing their names on the walls at the heads of their beds.

Dissolve to same scene next day (Saturday, April 7). Best has found an electric razor in his luggage, so the men are uncommonly groomed. There is general agreement that the main anxieties are now safely past. Bonhoeffer and Kokorin, back sunning themselves again, are wondering about their friendship and their future. This dialogue may be the best chance left to suggest some of the last ideas we have from Bonhoeffer. His Tegel letters, before they were stopped, had spoken enigmatically of a "non-religious interpretation of the Gospel" and a "religionless Christianity." Now here he sits with an ideal citizen of the world come of age, a contemporary who has never had recourse to the "God hypothesis," but who shares a prison with Bonhoeffer because they have stood for some of the same things, and resisted the same threat to humanity. We can only guess what language Bonhoeffer would have used to go beyond superficialities with the young communist. But each in his own way would probably hail the resourceful new world that was developing, with its abundance and its possibilities and its answering of old questions. Each would have celebrated his humanity and wondered what it meant to be a man in a world on its own. They must have concurred in emphases on freedom, justice, peace, though details would differ, as they would on gratitude and hope. And both would have been for risking action. Basic faiths may differ, but common enterprise is in order. At which point we may even hazard an interpretation of Bonhoeffer's unelucidated reference to a "secret discipline." Might not this refer to a conceptual coexistence, a *private* reflection and devotion of the likeminded, a believing community's non-aggressive exploration of its own deeps, more for special motivation to common endeavor than for defining a separate identity?

If so, the conversation could end with Bonhoeffer's, *And you and I must compare and contrast such private thinking when there is time, because it is about what each of us claims is real and true.* Kokorin, apprehensive of the preacher, *But we will not club each other with these private claims?* Bonhoeffer gets sly, *No, but each will check on the other and speak up if the other is betraying his own claim—as I will say you are cheating if you, who by your own lights are for justice for all, should start claiming it mostly for Russia.* Kokorin is just as sly, *And as I will say you are cheating if you, who claim among yourselves to live for love of the world, should start pushing again mainly for the church.* Bonhoeffer says, *Fair enough; and isn't the sun glorious?*

The slashing cut is to Adolf Hitler, slamming a notebook onto his desk, in his command bunker. It is Canaris' diary, just ferreted out, and it is explicit about every participant in every plot. Hitler is just as specific. Everyone mentioned who is still alive is to be executed at once: He has a short list of conspirators who must "under no circumstances be allowed to live."

Cut to a prison hospital in Berlin. A sympathetic doctor has alerted Christine, and she is with Hans for a last few minutes. While she is there the doctor drugs Hans very heavily, hoping even yet to make him unfit for a sentencing court. Sonderegger, who arrives to get Hans, is contemptuous. Shortly after, at Sachsenhausen, the half-conscious Hans von Dohnanyi, collapsed on his stretcher, is sentenced to death.

Elsewhere, a Nazi officer gets secret orders, leads a column of cars out of Berlin, headed for Flossenbürg. Bonhoeffer's trial judge and the judge's wife are in one of the cars, he to give a veneer of legal formality to the summary court, she to escape the disintegrating capital. About the same time an SS judge leaves Nuremberg in a freight train, rides a bicycle the last twenty kilometers from Weiden to Flossenbürg. All arrive at the bare, gray room in the concentration camp laundry room that will be their court. Schlabrendorff, Müller, Liedig are led in. *Where is Bonhoeffer?* Fury. Guards shout at Liedig, *You* are *Bonhoeffer*. The judge snaps orders to get Dietrich Bonhoeffer at once.

Sunday morning, April 8, 1945. The school room at Schönberg—sunny, quiet; deep content. A friend goes to Bonhoeffer, who is leaning out the window, and asks if he will lead in morning prayer. Bonhoeffer gets the inquirer to lean out the window too, so he can explain his reluctance: *Please, when we have only each other, let us not do anything to bring up the old divisions. I am a Protestant, most of the others are Catholic, and then there is Kokorin; I cannot offend him.* But the others rebuke Bonhoeffer: You *are bringing up the divisions; please don't raise those flimsy fences again.* And Kokorin comes to lean out with him: *I would be glad to go to morning prayer with you.*

So a simple service is devised. In his old Finkenwalde way, Dietrich prays colloquially, directly: thanksgiving for life, for each other, for the day; repentance for whatever offences; and low, almost whispered, slow intercessions for the families, the troops, comrades, the countries. The Bible readings for the day are short, "Through his stripes are we healed" (Isaiah 53:5) and "Praise be to God and the Father of our Lord Jesus Christ, who in his great mercy has raised us to a living hope through the resurrection of Jesus Christ from the dead" (I Peter 1:3). The brief sermon given to him in the film could develop a true and fitting summary from the two texts. It might begin almost apologetically: *How much easier it would have been to preach on these texts a few years ago. What language I could have used; universal wounds and cosmic mendings, and I would have known what I meant then, I hope, but now I can't remember. For what we have is one whom Isaiah calls the Suffering Servant, and he has been whipped. For us, it says; of course for us, he was always for others. And so we believe God is for others, and so we say we should be for others. Whipped, if need be; surely, whipped— for others. Neither God nor Jesus Christ nor you nor I are lordly and powerful and lifted up. All of us are in the middle of things, taking what we must for each other. But not glumly, oh not glumly!! For there is the other text too about the wide open future. Death is a door that has been slammed back against the wall. That makes a difference to us right now.* And this idea might be completed in line with a paragraph from the *Ethics,* p. 17. "But wherever it is recognized that the power of death has been broken . . . there no eternities are demanded of life but one takes of life what it offers, not all or nothing, but good *and* evil, the important *and* the unimportant, joy *and* sorrow; one neither clings convulsively to life nor casts it frivolously away. One is content with the allotted span and one does not invest earthly things with the title of eternity; one allows death the limited rights which it still possesses."

Immediately after the service a child slips in from the rooms where the families are jailed, and Dietrich, delighted to be plotting with youth again, begins funny plans to smuggle himself down the hall to repeat the morning prayer for the others. The laughter is mounting as others offer unlikely possibilities, and then the door crashes open, two nondescript but menacing civilians step just inside, and say, *Prisoner Bonhoeffer, get ready and come with us.* The phrase is a dread formula; its significance is known to all prisoners. So hope dies, while mouths are still framed for laughing.

He puts his few effects in order. (The signing of his name in the Plutarch with which the film began, actually takes place at this time.) Going to the door, he passes Payne Best, pauses to send through him fond greeting and farewell to George Bell at Chichester, murmurs (according to Best) *This is the end, for me the beginning of life.* Then he runs down the stairs to the waiting car, lingering only another moment for a tearful embrace from Frau Goerdeler.

It is the ultimate insanity. Through the beautiful spring, by back roads they race north along the wafer-thin Berlin-Munich corridor which is all that is left in German control. To the east, the sound of Russian guns; to the west, American. In between, just these narrow roads through smiling fields, hastening streams and burbling rills, farm women at their planting, busy chickens scratching in the barnyard corners where the manure was stacked all winter against its current spreading (its ripeness fills the air most of the way for this funeral dash). Through ancient villages, past mouldering walls, old churches, worn and flaking shrines, crucifixes. Children playing on town doorsteps, glad in their springtime: coatless because summer is coming, stocking-capped because winter was here, snot-noses in sun-bright faces.

Is there talk? Bonhoeffer would never beg, least of all from such brutes as could obediently carry men back and forth to pointless death along the last, constricting corridor of a blasted state. But it would have been in character to ask his captors about themselves, about their families. And he could well have called attention to the enemy guns, sounding out of each side of the car. And the value of an "anchor in the future," a good word from a grateful beneficiary. At very least, the idiocy of this particular last gasp.

But they come, inexorably, to Flossenbürg. The town lies in the only ugly part of Bavaria. The land is flat, bleak, grim; the dark woods menace. Across the fields rises a single crag, and on it the ominous, crumbling ruin of a great castle. The Hohenstaufens built it a thousand years ago, lived in it six hundred years and now for the last four hundred years its broken walls have stood as cliffs, soaring architecture become gaunt geology. At the foot of the granite peak curls the gray little quarry town, and in it the slave labor camp where tens of thousands of political prisoners from occupied countries had been and are driven to death hacking at the frozen granite faces. Only since July 20, 1944, had Flossenbürg been used as an extermination camp (*systematic* extermination, that is, as over against the casual destruction of the conscripted who were simply worked to death). The dreary remoteness was just right for the condemned elite's liquidation, so here they were brought.

By evening the remorselessly efficient guards have reached the camp. The Mercedes, checked through the various fences and barriers, turns to the right inside the camp, away from the administration building and the slave barracks beyond. It is the prison barracks the driver heads for, with its long courtyard sealed back of high walls. This prime inscrutability is tucked back into a corner of the camp, half masked by the big laundry building that lies between it and the rest of the camp, and just a few hundred feet above the incinerator hut with its granite-slab table where two corpses at a time can have the gold and silver ripped from their mouths, and wheeled, iron stretchers wait to trundle flopping bodies into the furnace.

Bonhoeffer is turned over to other guards at the prison entrance, hurried across the courtyard and into the big room in the middle of the barracks which is itself the back wall of the yard. He confirms his identity, and is taken at once down the narrow hall which runs the full length of the barracks front, and along which the thick doors to tiny cells seal his listening, despairing friends. He is locked into his cell, with its iron cot, and its high, little, barred window opening on a twilight sky. The walls between the cells are thick and solid, even rapping is muffled. Beyond the massive doors with their little traps opened only from the outside, guards pace the narrow aisle. All the men there are alone.

Sometime in the night Bonhoeffer is marched back across the courtyard, through the wall, and over to the improvised courtroom in the laundry building. There is brief reunion with several others familiar from the earliest Abwehr adventures: Canaris, Oster, Sack, etc. There is no record of the summary court, but every reason to doubt its legality. From other conspirators' reports, it is more than likely that the increasingly desperate judges lunge once more for the moral superiority that earlier had buoyed them. The military men are chided for their treason. *And Pastor Bonhoeffer, you a Christian pastor, how could you reconcile your murderous design with your faith in God, the Ten Commandments, your preaching of love, your ordination and office?*

It is *the* question, of course. Whether the prisoners played for time, answered at length, explained themselves, is left to conjecture. With nothing left to defend but their dignity they may have secured that in silence. There is uncontrived occasion here, though, for a filmplay to summarize its moral argument.

By midnight the men are back in their cells; Canaris signals a neighbor that it is all over.

At dawn, we are back in the sequence that opened the film. There is no need to repeat it. Perhaps as Dietrich Bonhoeffer crosses the prison yard to the gallows his scene can be slowed and dimmed as on other parts of the screen Klaus and Rüdiger march to the Berlin wall where they are shot and Hans is carried to his execution. Then these scenes too may fade a little as Maria is found making her way from shattered city to shattered city, camp to camp, climbing through rubble, looking, asking, calling. . . . She did not find out until two months later what had happened to Dietrich, and then she couldn't get the word to Berlin.

His parents hoped for another whole month after that. Then, one night, dialing as usual for the BBC international broadcast, the parents and Eberhard and Renate Bethge tune in a memorial service already underway in London. Suddenly Vaughan Williams' mighty setting of "For All the Saints" fills the room. Then prayers. And at last the name of the honored dead: Dietrich Bonhoeffer. Then they know too.

In another church memorial service for wartime martyrs, held in Dietrich's homeland soon after hostilities were over, Bonhoeffer was not mentioned. Too political, said the preachers.

Liberties

nine months later than is here indicated, and in Berlin. But the Magdeburg Cathedral issue, already drawn at this earlier time, was being widely discussed.

pp. 102–103 Dietrich Bonhoeffer and Martin Niemöller were brought together in the German church struggle four months later (July, 1933) than is here indicated. The anticipation at this point is justified only as part of the effort to make swift sense of that bewildering complexity.

p. 105 The same streamlining attempt assigns Niemöller to receive Bonhoeffer's protest as here imagined. Actually, such a conversation in March 1933 would probably have been with Pastor Gerhard Jacobi, but it would also have been to the same effect.

pp. 120–122 The business about the visits to the Archbishop of Canterbury is not invented but *is* considerably reorganized here to illustrate the very real difference in the official reception given to Bonhoeffer and to Heckel. Bonhoeffer's first visit with the Archbishop antedated Heckel's visit to England. In fact, it was his report on German church developments which prompted the Archbishop to write President von Hindenburg in urgent inquiry and forceful protest about what was happening in Germany. Hindenburg was uneasy enough himself to pass the letter along to Chancellor Hitler, who, since Bonhoeffer's association with the letter was known, may thus have met the young man's name for the first time. Heckel's visit to London was, in fact, one consequence of the letter. He did get the brush-off there from the Archbishop, as here reported. And in high English councils Bonhoeffer

241

was already the trusted source of information on German events.

pp. 129–130   Hildebrandt's presence at opening day in Zingst is a *Memo* elision. He did look at many locations with Bonhoeffer, while the search for a seminary site was on. But he happens not to have been in on the discovery of Zingst. For that matter, Niesel might not have been on hand either, just the day here suggested. And student Koch actually arrived one term later. But surely simplification justifies such grouping?

pp. 137–138   The break with the girl he called Hannah (the name itself is a "Liberty") came not in a conversation but in a letter. The relationship as long as it lasted was one that would have been familiar to American students twenty-five years later. Campus activists, Dietrich and Hannah were joyously together in rallies, protests, campaigns. A theological student herself (and subsequently a distinguished churchwoman and scholar), Hannah worked with Dietrich on research projects. During the London interlude, Dietrich was prone to send her his sermons. There is reason to think that in connection with matrimony the exigencies of clandestine seminary existence were more daunting to Dietrich than they were to Hannah. Anyway, things were called off by mail.

p. 138   Fabian von Schlabrendorff actually met Bonhoeffer somewhat later—but this is the right place to pool these particular names.

p. 155   In the Schlawe parish, Bonhoeffer, Bethge, and friends lived first at Gross Schlönwitz (one and one-half years), and at Sigurdhof for the last year. But the Sigurdhof is more interesting, cinematically, and the move is not important, historically.

p. 157 The "take up the sword" speech is a paraphrase of a certifiable answer given by Bonhoeffer to Dohnanyi's honest question.

p. 159 The first "conspiracy" scene is contrived. Dietrich Bonhoeffer was in Pomerania at the time of the *Kristainscht*, and so would not have been available for the meeting with the Dohnanyis on the day suggested here. Furthermore, it is likely that he had been in *some* awareness of what was going on in Colonel Oster's Abwehr unit since Hans von Dohnanyi was brought into contact with that conspiratorial group earlier in 1936 while working on the Fritsch case (Hitler got rid of the recalcitrant General Fritsch by trumping up the usual homosexuality charges against him). Besides, Karl Barth's widely publicized letter to the Czech theologian, Josef Hromadka, had by this time released even the purest Barthians from their churchly fixation: Czech soldiers were hailed by Barth as "soldiers of Christ" in their violent resistance to Hitler. So discussions of the kind imagined in the *Memo* for November 1938, could as well have taken place anytime in the six months before. A crisis of decision was building in Bonhoeffer most of that year.

p. 166 As noted in the text, the personnel of the conspiratorial group meeting on surrender terms is the memo-writer's ad hoc. All the men mentioned, though, could have been in this group by this time, which is what matters to the narrative.

p. 168 The return to Bamberg cathedral was a

deliberate "liberty" on the writer's part. It fit so well, he invented it. Except that *after* its invention Eberhard Bethge confirmed that exactly such a visit did in fact take place, and that Dietrich Bonhoeffer did indeed comment on "how much smaller the medieval knight looks now than when we were children."

pp. 180–181 Hans Schönfeld was in Geneva when Bonhoeffer arrived, but was unavailable as he took off on the trip which Bonhoeffer would intersect later elsewhere.

p. 183 The love affair with Ruth von Wedemyer gets off to a much faster start in these pages than it did in fact. It was weeks, even months after this June encounter before Dietrich admitted to himself how attracted he was to Ruth. It was late fall before the families began to take the possibility of their marriage seriously. But with so little time to develop so intense a part of the Bonhoeffer story, the pace is deliberately forced here.

p. 188 The March 21, 1943 attempt on Hitler's life was to take place just after the dictator's visit to the Tomb of the Unknown Soldier. He was scheduled to visit a building near the Tomb, and there Major von Gersdorff waited with his bombs. But, as was to happen so often during the plotting, Hitler abridged his schedule and extended his life. He didn't stop next door. This happened too often in Hitler's last years to be uncanny impulse. It was undoubtedly the very canny strategy of a tyrant who knew himself hated and hunted.

p. 189 The reassuring word from Admiral Canaris actually came through five days after the birthday party, and if it came by phone it could only have been very guarded. This also means that Dietrich Bonhoeffer's call to Christine was a few days later than here indicated.

p. 190   The story of the ancestors' meeting in prison is true. There is no evidence that it was remembered as suggested here, though there is no reason why it couldn't have been. Dr. Bethge vouches for the history and for the presence of the books in the study, but doesn't remember any such moment.

p. 196   All we know for sure is that Bonhoeffer was critical of the crust, revolted by the blankets.

p. 205   The idea that Roeder charges Sonderegger to more vigorous sleuthing at this point is completely deductive.

pp. 207–208   The prison conversations are completely imaginary. General von Hase is dead. Eberhard Bethge and Ruth von Wedemyer have some memories they need not share with us. So the occasions are used here to bruit ideas otherwise hard to get in.

p. 214   Eberhard Bethge was arrested two weeks later, by wire. As clerk to his commanding officer at the Italian front, he opened and read the wire first ("bring Bethge to Berlin under heavy guard") —and delivered it. There was no choice. Renate and the baby were defenseless in Berlin.

p. 215   Early readers of the *Memo* questioned the facticity of these shower-room scenes. They seemed too obviously contrived for the current nudity kick in this film era. They are, however, stark truth.

p. 215   A Judge Huppenkothen was in charge of prosecuting Hans and Dietrich. Sonderegger assisted him. But Sonderegger by now should be known to viewers,

and the story doesn't need another name
in its already staggering cast. Besides,
the Huppenkothens shouldn't object to
being left out.

p. 218   Dietrich did finally meet Hans in the
circumstances described. And Hans was
in bad shape. But secretly he was practicing walking. He intended to be ready
to leave when it was time to leave.

pp. 233–234   The scripture lessons for the day are
certain. The prayers and the sermon
are pure conjecture.

p. 235   Payne Best reports longer farewell remarks, including references to the ecumenical church and greetings to Bishop
Bell. People remember what they remember, of course, but Best's full report
is somehow too oracular for Bonhoeffer.
Even the famous "this is the end, for
me the beginning . . ." is not exactly
in character. But it is too well-known,
too widely admired to challenge now—
especially on no contrary documentation at all.

p. 239   It is not known how the helpless Hans
von Dohnanyi was killed.

Cast

Barth, Karl (1884–1966), Swiss, virtuoso theologian, professor at Universities of Göttingen, Münster, Bonn, and Basle. Spiritual leader of the European Resistance after 1938.

Beck, Colonel General Ludwig (1880–1944), chief of the German General Staff in the middle 1930's, and already then as in his subsequent retirement the leading figure and moral center of anti-Nazi resistance. Executed in 1944.

Bell, Dr. George Kennedy (1883–1958), the bishop of Chichester; close friend of Dietrich Bonhoeffer from London interlude on; a leading architect of the World Council of Churches and later chairman of its Central Committee, then honorary president of the Council.

Best, Capt. Payne, member of British Secret Service, lured to German-Dutch border and captured there by Nazis in what came to be called the "Venlo Incident." The incident was important for its braking effect on German Opposition attempts to get the British to take the Resistance seriously. Best was at Buchenwald with Bonhoeffer.

Bethge, Eberhard, author, theologian, educator, church statesman; at first Dietrich Bonhoeffer's student, then his most intimate companion and colleague; Bonhoeffer's literary executor, and principal source for all succeeding Bonhoeffer studies.

————, *Renate*, daughter of Ursula (Bonhoeffer) and Rüdiger Schleicher; wife of Eberhard Bethge; niece of Dietrich Bonhoeffer.

Bonhoeffer, Karl, the father, professor of psychiatry and nervous diseases at the University of Berlin; director of Dept. of Psychiatry at Charité Hospital.

————, *Paula* (born von Hase), the mother.

Bonhoeffer, Karl Friedrich, oldest son (b. Jan. 1899); physicist; husband of Greta von Dohnanyi.

————,*Walter*, second son (b. Dec. 1899); killed in World War I.

————, *Klaus*, third son (b. 1901); lawyer; husband of Emmi Delbrück.

————, *Ursula*, eldest daughter (b. 1902); married to Rüdiger Schleicher.

————, *Christine* (also called Christel), second daughter (b. 1903); married to Hans von Dohnanyi.

————, *Dietrich*, fourth son (b. 1906); theologian; twin to Sabine.

————, *Sabine*, third daughter (b. 1906); Dietrich's twin; married to Gerhard Leibholz.

————, *Susanne*, fourth daughter (b. 1909); married to Walter Dress.

Brauchitsch, Colonel General (later, Field Marshal) *Walther von* (1881–1948), Commander in Chief of Army; generally negative about Resistance (his wife was fanatically pro-Nazi); but also worried by Hitler's military designs; comes closest to cooperating with opposition in 1938.

Canaris, Admiral Walter-Wilhelm (1885–1945), enigmatic head of the Abwehr (military secret service) who housed, encouraged, and aided the Resistance —and stayed in close touch with the Nazi leaders most dangerous to him; a manager of espionage and counter-espionage, he was made ill by violence of any kind; a fatalist, he contrived to steer events; a fascinating little man, an incessant world traveler, given to great physical daring; a mystery through and through; executed, 1945.

Crinis, Dr. Max de, psychiatrist, successor to Dr. Karl Bonhoeffer on the University of Berlin faculty.

Delbrück, Emmi, daughter of historian, Hans Delbrück; sister of Justus Delbrück; wife of Klaus Bonhoeffer.

————, *Justus*, son of Hans Delbrück; brother of Emmi Delbrück Bonhoeffer; lawyer; close friend of Klaus Bonhoeffer.

Dibelius, Otto, German churchman; subsequently bishop of Berlin.

CAST

Dohnanyi, Christine (Bonhoeffer) *von*, Dietrich Bonhoeffer's sister, wife of Hans von Dohnanyi.

————, *Greta von*, daughter of composer Ernst von; sister of Hans von, wife of Karl Friedrich Bonhoeffer.

————, *Hans von*, son of Ernst von; brother of Greta; husband of Christine Bonhoeffer; Supreme Court jurist; later, Abwehr official.

Dress, Walter, church historian, husband of Susanne Bonhoeffer.

Fisher, Frank (b. 1908), undergraduate student at Union seminary in 1931; intimate of Dietrich Bonhoeffer, whom he introduced to his Harlem home, church, and culture; died young.

Freisler, Roland, fanatically Nazi judge, president of the "peoples court."

Gersdorff, Major Baron Rudolf von, youthful officer who proposed to destroy Hitler and himself with bombs, if the fateful adjacency could be contrived.

Goerdeler, Carl (1884–1944), highly regarded former mayor of Leipzig; chief conservative philosopher of the Resistance, its wide-ranging and imperturbable courier, its most dangerously open and verbal exponent; would have been Chancellor in any Resistance-established government.

Haeften, Hans von, childhood friend of Dietrich Bonhoeffer, later in diplomatic service of Germany.

Halder, Colonel General Franz (b. 1884), successor to General Ludwig Beck as chief of the General Staff; generally sympathetic to the Resistance, but on and off in his cooperation, with his own unpredictable resistances.

Hammerstein-Equord, Colonel General Baron Kurt von (1878–1943), Commander in Chief of the German Army before 1934; an anti-Nazi from the beginning (sometimes called "the red general" by critical colleagues; on Hammerstein's palette, Nazis were "brown scum"); briefly reactivated for the Polish campaign, he tried desperately to lure Hitler into a trap, but failed.

Harnack, Adolf (1851–1930), German liberal theologian, famed historian of Chrisian ideas, teacher of Dietrich Bonhoeffer at the University of Berlin.

CAST

Hase, Hans-Cristoph von (b. 1907), pastor, cousin of
Dietrich Bonhoeffer, and of about the same age.

————, *Paul von* (1885–1944), lieutenant general,
military commander of Berlin region, long-unsus-
pected member of anti-Nazi conspiracy; cousin of
Dietrich Bonhoeffer's mother, Paula von Hase
Bonhoeffer.

Hassell, Ulrich von (1881–1944), anti-Nazi diplomat,
diarist.

Heckel, Theodor, functionary at foreign relations desk
of the German state church; later, bishop.

Hildebrand, Franz, theologian, early friend of Dietrich
Bonhoeffer, with whom he was closely associated
at the beginning of the church struggle and during
the London interlude.

Horn, Käthe, governess, especially to the young twins,
Dietrich and Sabine.

————, *Maria*, governess in Bonhoeffer home, sister
of Käthe.

Kalkreuth, the Countess Christine, Munich artist,
Dietrich Bonhoeffer's aunt; daughter of artist
Count Leopold Kalkreuth.

Kleist-Retzow, Ruth von (1867–1945), born the Countess of Zedlitz-Trützschler, matriarch of solid,
landed family; earnest, informed churchwoman;
a main supporter of Dietrich Bonhoeffer, from
Finkenwalde days on; grandmother of Bonhoeffer's
fiancee, Maria von Wedemeyer; mother of Hans
Jürgen von Kleist-Retzow.

————, *Hans Jürgen*, distinguished landholder, active anti-Nazi.

Kleist-Schmenzin, Ewald von (1890–1945), large land-
owner.

Kluge, Colonel General (later, Field Marshal) *Ewald
von*, a leading general, attentive to the Opposition.

Koch, Werner (b. 1910), a student in the second class
convened at Finkenwalde (1935); prisoner at
Sachsenhausen (1936–38); now a pastor.

Kokorin, Vassily, Russian aviator, nephew of Foreign
Minister Molotov of the Soviet Union (Molotov's
relatives were his best feature: he was himself a
nephew of the composer, Scriabine); fellow
prisoner with Dietrich Bonhoeffer in Nazi camps.

Lassère, Jean (b. 1906), French pastor, pacifist, fellow-student with Dietrich Bonhoeffer at Union Seminary, 1931.

Lehmann, Paul (b. 1906), American theologian, close friend of Dietrich Bonhoeffer at Union Seminary (1931) and during subsequent visits to Germany; associated with Reinhold Niebuhr in engineering Bonhoeffer's 1939 trip to New York.

Leuschner, Wilhelm, prominent moderate Social Democrat, and the last president of the Free Trade Unions before their suppression by the Nazis; joined Beck and Goerdeler in the Opposition's top echelons.

Liebholz, Gerhard, youngest professor of law at Göttingen University; professor on law faculty at Oxford University after escape from Germany; on return, after the war, restored to Göttingen professorship, and became a Justice of the Supreme Court of West Germany; husband of Sabine Bonhoeffer (Dietrich's twin).

Liedig, Capt. Franz, member of the Abwehr resistance ring; with Bonhoeffer at Buchenwald.

Moltke, Count Helmut von (1907–1945), organizer of a second Resistance center, the "Kreisan Circle" (named for the Moltke estate), of exceedingly reflective and idealistic conspirators.

Müller, Dr. Joseph, Roman Catholic lawyer, based in Munich; one of the Abwehr conspiracy's principal agents, especially useful in its repeated contacts with the Pope, who gave Müller his full confidence and cooperation.

Müller, Reichsbishop Ludwig (1883–1946), exceedingly limited military chaplain friend of Adolf Hitler in their youth; elevated to an inappropriate supremacy in German state church by Der Führer.

Niebuhr, Reinhold (b. 1892), theologian, professor of social ethics at Union Theological Seminary; Gifford Lecturer.

Niemöller, Martin (b. 1890), German pastor, a leader of the break-away Confessing church, imprisoned by Nazi government; more recently, a president of the World Council of Churches.

Niesel, Wilhelm, German theologian, a leader in the Confessing church; Calvin scholar; later, president of the World Reformed Alliance.

Oster, Major General Hans, in direct charge (under Admiral Canaris) of the department within the Abwehr which engineered and pressed the principal plots against the Nazi state before 1944; executed, 1945.

Rabenau, General Friedrich von (1884–1945), retired chief librarian of German army, a late arrival to theological studies; involved in Resistance; cellmate of Dietrich Bonhoeffer at Buchenwald.

Roeder, Manfred, chief investigator for the Air Force.

Rose, Dr. Eugen, pastor, member of Finkenwalde student group that went to Sweden with Dietrich Bonhoeffer.

Rott, Wilhelm (b. 1908), assistant to Dietrich Bonhoeffer at Finkenwalde (1935–1937); subsequently worked for Abwehr; more recently, church superintendent in Koblenz.

Sack, Dr. Karl, lawyer, military advocate-general; well-covered member of the Resistance; executed, 1945.

Sauerbruch, Dr. Ferdinand, world famed surgeon, head of Berlin's great Charité Hospital, colleague of Karl Bonhoeffer.

Schacht, Hjalmar (b. 1877), minister of economics in the Nazi government, but an incredible vacillator; he aided the conspiracy from time to time, which is also how he enjoyed Hitler's favor.

Schlabrendorff, Fabian von (b. 1907), lawyer, leader in Resistance, involved in attempt on Hitler's life; prisoner with Dietrich Bonhoeffer at Flossenbürg.

Schleicher, Rüdiger (1901–1945), lawyer, Resistance figure; husband of Ursula Bonhoeffer; father of Renate Schleicher Bethge, wife of Eberhard Bethge.

Schönfeld, Dr. Hans, German state church representative to ecumenical committees (pre-World Council of Churches) in Geneva; he was, as such, no early champion of the Confessing church, but he did emerge much later as an emissary for the Kreisau Circle of anti-Nazi conspirators.

Sonderegger, Franz, Gestapo agent.

Stauffenberg, Count Claus Schenk (1904–1944), brilliant young army officer who sparked and managed the last round of conspiratorial activity, culminating in the abortive July 20, 1944, attempt on Hitler's life, for which Stauffenberg was immediately executed.

Sutz, Erwin (b. 1907), Swiss pastor, Union Seminary student with Dietrich Bonhoeffer, 1931; helpful to Bonhoeffer during conspiratorial years.

Tillich, Ernst, pastor; nephew of theologian Paul Tillich; student at the University of Berlin when Bonhoeffer began teaching there in 1932; delegate with Bonhoeffer to Fanø Conference; active in church opposition to Nazis.

Visser 't Hooft, Dr. William A. (b. 1900), church statesman; Dutch; Barthian theologian; ecumenical pioneer; first General Secretary of the World Council of Churches, 1948–1966.

Wedemeyer, Maria von (b. 1924), fiancee of Dietrich Bonhoeffer; granddaughter of Bonhoeffer's friend and steady supporter, Ruth von Kleist-Retzow.

―――, *Ruth von,* mother of Maria von Wedemeyer, daughter of Ruth von Kleist-Retzow.

Weissler, Friedrich, lawyer, in service of the Confessing Church; died under torture at hands of the state.

Winterhager, Jürgen, student of Dietrich Bonhoeffer at the University of Berlin in 1932 (with Wolf-Dieter Zimmermann, a member of a "Bonhoeffer circle") and at Finkenwalde in 1936; participant in the church struggle.

Zimmermann, Wolf-Dieter (b. 1911), student of Dietrich Bonhoeffer at the University of Berlin in 1932 and at Finkenwalde in 1936; participant in the church struggle; now broadcasting executive for church in Berlin.

Credits

This *Memo for a Movie* was written specifically to introduce movie producers or directors to the fascinating figure of Dietrich Bonhoeffer, in the hope that an artist among film makers might be moved to make a true picture of the man and his significance.

Although in preparing this *Memo* the author consulted numerous sources relating to the life of Bonhoeffer, he gratefully and admiringly acknowledges Eberhard Bethge's enormous, exhaustive biography, *Dietrich Bonhoeffer* (Christian Kaiser Verlag, Munich, 1967; Harper and Row, New York, 1969; Collins, Ltd., London, 1969), as the most significant repository of the facts of Bonhoeffer's life. All studies of Bonhoeffer will, of necessity, owe a great debt to Mr. Bethge. This author, however, is particularly indebted to Dr. and Mrs. Bethge who regularly responded with suggestions, no matter how inopportune the importunate appeal. No one but the *Memo*-writer, of course, is responsible for the details and the interpretations as written. That means he gets the blame for whatever is blameworthy. He will gladly settle for whatever credit the Bethges will smile on to him!

The ensuing notes are an almost page-by-page acknowledgment of sources and references to further reading. Since the principal target for the *Memo* is still the English-speaking film maker, material in English is the main reference here. That means, especially, that the Collected Writings of Dietrich Bonhoeffer (*Gesammelte Schriften*, 4 volumes, edited by Eberhard Bethge, Chr. Kaiser Verlag, Munich, 1958–1961) will be cited wherever possible from the selections published in England and America as *No Rusty Swords* (edited by E. H. Robertson; Harper and Row, New York, 1965) and *The Way to Freedom* (edited by E. H. Robertson; Harper and Row, New York, 1966). Eberhard Bethge's biography, *Dietrich Bonhoeffer* (Chr. Kaiser Verlag, Munich, 1967), will have to be referred to in the pagination of the German original, since it had not appeared in English at the time these notes were made.

Abbreviations to be used for the most frequently cited titles are:

DB/EB	*Dietrich Bonhoeffer*, a biography, by Eberhard Bethge, Chr. Kaiser Verlag, Munich, second edition, 1967.
GS	*Gesammelte Schriften*, Dietrich Bonhoeffer, 4 volumes, Chr. Kaiser Verlag, Munich, 1958–1961. (The Collected Writings of Dietrich Bonhoeffer, edited by Eberhard Bethge—most of the writing is in German, but some letters and sermons are in Bonhoeffer's own English.)
IKDB	*I Knew Dietrich Bonhoeffer*, reminiscences by his friends, edited by Wolf-Dieter Zimmermann and Ronald Gregor Smith, translated by Käthe Gregor Smith, Harper and Row, New York, 1966.
LP	*Letters and Papers from Prison*, Dietrich Bonhoeffer, edited by Eberhard Bethge, translated by Reginald Fuller and others; Macmillan, New York, 1967 (revised and enlarged third edition).
NRS	*No Rusty Swords*, Dietrich Bonhoeffer, selections from the *Gesammelte Schriften*, edited by Edwin Robertson, translated by John Bowden, Harper and Row, New York, 1965.
TWTF	*The Way to Freedom*, Dietrich Bonhoeffer, more selections from *Gesammelte Schriften*, edited by Edwin Robertson, who also translated with John Bowden, Harper and Row, New York, 1966.
VEU	*Vergangen Erlebt Überwunden*, by Sabine Leibholz-Bonhoeffer, Johannes Kiefel Verlag, Wuppertal, 1968 (second edition).
pp. 22–23	"The Last Things and the Things Before Last": *Ethics*, Dietrich Bonhoeffer,

edited by Eberhard Bethge, translated by Neville Horton Smith, Macmillan, New York, 1955; pp. 79–141.

pp. 34f. description of parents and siblings: VEU, pp. 13–68; DB/EB, pp. 36–43; IKDB, pp. 19–37 (essays by Sabine Leibholz-Bonhoeffer and Emmi Delbrück Bonhoeffer).

pp. 35–41 itinerary for wandering: IKDB, pp. 25 and 31; DB/EB, p. 73; VEU, pp. 54–55.

p. 36 "Gute Ruh": IKBD, p. 27; VEU, p. 55; DB/EB, p. 48.

p. 39 DB as "knight": IKBD, p. 27; VEU, p. 53.

——— childhood stories: IKBD, pp. 22–29.

——— embarrassing self-analyses: DB/EB, pp. 63–66.

——— interest in pills and potions: emphasized in separate conversations with Eberhard and Renate Bethge, Erwin Sutz, Paul Lehmann.

p. 41 the home: IKDB, pp. 20ff., also p. 36; DB/EB, pp. 46–48, 51–53; VEU, pp. 55–56.

p. 42 the annuity episode: DB/EB, p. 74 (from Karl Friedrich Bonhoeffer's Memoirs).

p. 43 the circle of friends: IKDB, p. 30; DB/EB, pp. 52–53; VEU, p. 56.

——— the parties: IKDB, pp. 26, 27, 30; VEU, p. 56.

pp. 44–45 Bonhoeffer as one of "the little ones": emphasized in conversations with Dr. and Mrs. Bethge, and Prof. and Mrs. Leibholz.

——— the home, not "church": DB/EB, pp. 59–60; another emphasis in conversation with Dr. and Mrs. Bethge.

p. 50 the Horn sisters: IKDB, pp. 24–25; DB/EB, pp. 47, 59.

——— Klaus and "lights out": DB/EB, p. 60.

p. 51 Walter's death: GS, vol. I, p. 68 (a reminiscence by Bonhoeffer, in his own English); IKDB, p. 30; DB/EB, p. 50; VEU, pp. 33–36.

——— confirmation class: IKDB, pp. 30–31; DB/EB, p. 61.

————— General Booth: IKDB, p. 31.

p. 52 father's and brothers' "careful agnosticism": generally remarked by Bonhoeffer relatives and friends; Eberhard Bethge's essay in *World Come of Age* (ed., Ronald Gregor Smith, Fortress, Philadelphia, 1967), p. 32; also Bethge's essays in *Bonhoeffer in a World Come of Age* (ed. Peter Vorkink II, Fortress, 1968), pp. 82–83; also G. van Rad in IKDB, 176–177; also DB/EB, pp. 67–69.

————— the doctoral thesis, *Sanctorum Communio*, is available in English translation as *The Communion of the Saints*, Harper and Row, New York, 1963; Wm. Collins and Sons, London, 1963.

pp. 53–58 the theologies epitomized by the author were taught first to him in classrooms in New York, Zürich, and Basel, where he was a student of Reinhold Niebuhr, Paul Tillich, Emil Brunner, and Karl Barth; see especially, Theodore A. Gill, *Some Recent Protestant Political Thinking*, Hunt, Barnard, London, 1953, pp. 65–115.

p. 54 Bonhoeffer affected by his great liberal teachers: E. Bethge in *World Come of Age*, p. 32.

p. 55 the Barth quote is from his *Word of God and Word of Man*, a book of early essays.

p. 57 Bonhoeffer family and Barth: DB/EB, p. 104.

p. 58 Bonhoeffer's uncritical defense of Barth: NRS (app. II), pp. 361–372.

————— arrival at Tübingen: DB/EB, pp. 73–76.

p. 59 the Tübingen scenes depend most on Dr. Berend Wellmann, who read German with the author, was himself a Tübingen "Igel" full of recollections (c. 1965!), and who called attention to the Tübingen university atmosphere recreated by Thomas Mann for early chapters of his novel, *Dr. Faustus*.

p. 60 Bonhoeffer's certainty: DB/EB, p. 77.

————— politics: summarized in DB/EB, p.

78; Ludendorff-Hitler putsch described in the political history preferred by the *Memo*-writer, *Hitler: A Study in Tyranny*, Alan Bullock, Harper and Row, New York, 1962 (revised edition), pp. 106–113; see also Richard Hughes' novel, *The Fox in the Attic*, Harper and Row, New York, 1961, esp. pp. 159–226; also see Bonhoeffer himself on Versailles in GS, vol. I, pp. 70–73 (Bonhoeffer's own English).

————   beer church: Dr. Wellmann supplied the denomination.

p. 61   accompanying, hand-reading, etc.: DB/EB, pp. 76–77.

p. 62   "army" experiences: DB/EB, pp. 77–80.

pp. 62–63   Tübingen teachers: DB/EB, pp. 80–83.

————   skating accident: IKDB, p. 32.

pp. 63–64   Rome: Bonhoeffer's "little diary" quoted in DB/EB, pp. 85–88: Colliseum, Vatican, Laocoon, Apollo, Pan, St. Peters, Trinita vespers, Santa Maria Maggiore, Pincio (p. 67).

p. 65   response to Roman Catholicism: DB/EB, pp. 87–90.

p. 67   African adventure: DB/EB, pp. 86–87.

p. 68   University of Berlin faculty introduced: DB/EB, pp. 95–101.

p. 69   a tardily detected "liberty": Harnack's suggestion that Bonhoeffer pursue church history came in a 1925 afternoon seminar; Bonhoeffer, much set up, went from there to a performance of the St. Matthew Passion—and remembered that excitement in 1943, when, in Tegel Prison, he heard the Passion again on the radio; NRS, pp. 27–31, has exchanges between Harnack and Bonhoeffer in the earlier period; it should also be admitted that young colleague Wellmann was dubious about this author's idea that a German professor and a student should be seen speaking so informally in public!

pp. 69–70   the pot lid image is remembered from Eduard Thurneysen's preaching.

p. 71   the Bible stories: DB/EB, p. 123.

       the door opened from the other side: Maria von Wedemeyer-Weller, *Bonhoeffer in a World Come of Age*, p. 110.

pp. 71–73   the scene is a free invention, but is not unrelated to the correspondence with R. Widemann reported in DB/EB, pp. 124–125.

pp. 74–76   Spain: NRS, 34–39; DB/EB, pp. 136–138.

       the Barcelona vicar: DB/EB, pp. 138–144.

       the scruple about "principles": NRS, pp. 39–48 (comprising a lecture "What Is a Christian Ethic"), see especially p. 45.

p. 77   Don Quixote: DB/EB, p. 134.

       Gandhi trip: DB/EB, p. 138.

       new atmosphere in Germany: for background, required reading is Peter Gay, *Weimar Culture*, Harper and Row, New York, 1968; also William Sheridan Allen's *The Nazi Seizure of Power* (the experience of a single German town, 1930–1935), Quadrangle Books, Chicago, 1935; also, Alan Bullock, *Hitler*, pp. 151–186.

       second book: *Akt und Sein*, translated as *Act and Being* (trans. by Bernard Noble), Harper and Row, New York, 1962.

p. 78   Harnack funeral speech: NRS, pp. 29–31.

       Bonhoeffer's inaugural address ("Man in Contemporary Philosophy and Theology"): NRS, pp. 50–69.

       Hildebrandt: DB/EB, pp. 174–175. (Hildebrandt himself has written little about Bonhoeffer; in conversation he has spoken for all Bonhoeffer friends and relatives: "Eberhard Bethge has told superbly all there is to tell.")

p. 79   Erwin Sutz: dormitory and Mexican trip details come from conversations with Dr. Sutz.

       classes at Union: NRS, pp. 89–91; DB/EB, pp. 193f.

p. 79   DB on crisis theology: GS, vol. III, pp. 110–136.

――――   Niebuhr's line: described on the basis of Niebuhr's lectures attended by the author a few years later.

p. 80   friends: IKDB, pp. 46–51 (E. Bethge), pp. 4–45 (P. Lehmann); DB/EB, pp. 189–193.

――――   the issue of Bonhoeffer's "pacifism": IKDB, p. 47; DB/EB, p. 90.

――――   Harlem: IKDB, p. 49.

――――   tennis: IKDB, p. 43.

――――   Cuba: DB/EB, p. 188.

p. 82   cross country trip: DB/EB, pp. 188–189; further elaborated on the strength of conversations with Erwin Sutz and Paul Lehmann.

p. 84   summary of attitudes on U.S. church: NRS, pp. 86–91; amplified on strength of international students' standard impressions.

――――   the Negro question: NRS, pp. 112–114 (1939); DB/EB, p. 187.

――――   Barth seminar: description built on author's own experience in Dr. Barth's seminars in Basle (1946–1948).

――――   Luther quote: DB/EB, p. 216.

p. 85   "check on fingernails": DB/EB, p. 217.

――――   Gunther Dehn case: Cochrane, *The Church's Confession Under Hitler*, pp. 51–53.

p. 86   Barth pronouncement: *Theologische Existenz Heute*, June 25, 1933; see Cochrane, pp. 102–104.

p. 87   the "impetuous," "cautious" disjunction: the words are E. Bethge's, DB/EB, p. 224; see also Bonhoeffer's letters, NRS, pp. 119–122.

pp. 90–94   German politics in years preceding the Nazi takeover: Gay, Allen, Bullock, all previously cited, plus Milton Mayer, *They Thought They Were Free*, U. of Chicago, Chicago, 1955; see also Bonhoeffer's letters, NRS, pp. 123–124.

p. 95   "forty-year-old" remark: Peter Gay (pp. 142–143) quoting Jacob Wassermann;

Richard Freedman's remark in *Book World*, Nov. 24, 1968, p. 7.

p. 97 ecumenical meetings: DB/EB, pp. 232–246 and 286–304; also, in Bonhoeffer's correspondence and papers, NRS, pp. 135–139 and 157–189.

p. 98 confirmation class: DB/EB, pp. 272–275; NRS, pp. 139–141 and 149–152; IKDB, pp. 55–58 and 65–66.

——— new catechism: NRS, pp. 141–149.

pp. 100–101 aborted radio talk: NRS, pp. 190–204; DB/EB, pp. 307–309.

p. 102 history of the church struggle: see especially Conway, *The Nazi Persecution of the Churches 1933–1945*, and Cochrane; also NRS, pp. 204–234 (letters, sermons, statements, June–Sept. 1933).

——— "culture known by its exiles": R. Freedman's remark, op. cit.

pp. 102–103 Dr. Bonhoeffer and Reichstag's inquiry: DB/EB, p. 313.

p. 106 Barth on waiting for "a more central issue": NRS, p. 232; DB/EB, pp. 362–363; see also NRS, pp. 221–234 for Bonhoeffer's attitudes, and letter exchange with Barth; Jewish issue as essential issue to Bonhoeffer; *World Come of Age*, pp. 48–49; Jewish issue as personal; DB/EB, pp. 325–326.

p. 107 Reformation Day sermon: in English (trans. by Lewis Wilkins), *MSS*, vol. 1, no. 4, April 1970 (T. A. Gill, editor); commented on, DB/EB, p. 285.

p. 108 Grandmother Bonhoeffer episode: VEU, p. 96; DB/EB, p. 316.

——— P. Lehmann's observation: DB/EB, p. 313; repeated in conversation.

p. 109 church developments: Cochrane, pp. 90–139; DB/EB, pp. 304–374.

——— strike idea: DB/EB, p. 361; recalled in conversation with F. Hildebrandt, also.

p. 110 Bethel: NRS, pp. 240–242 (comment on the sections on Jewish question); DB/EB, pp. 352–357.

pp. 111–112 Heckel and London idea: DB/EB, pp.

375–378; the ambiguities are reinforced here in response to E. Bethge's suggestion in conversations.

p. 117   London household: IKDB, pp. 77–81 (Zimmermann and Whitburn); DB/EB, pp. 381–383.

p. 118   Barth's letter: NRS, pp. 234–240 (the brisk exchange).

———   Barmen: Cochrane, pp. 129–263; DB/EB, pp. 424–428 and 430.

pp. 118–119   the issue of recognizing the Confessing Church ecumenically: GS, vol. I, pp. 230–239 (a letter exchange with Prof. Hodgson illustrates issue); DB/EB, pp. 416–418.

———   Bethge's analysis of ecumenical opportunity: DB/EB, p. 428; see also Bonhoeffer's summary, NRS, pp. 326–344.

———   anti-Nazi and parish activities in London: DB/EB, pp. 386–402; also letters, NRS, pp. 250–278.

p. 120   Heckel in London: DB/EB, pp. 402–411; Lambeth details from author's own visit to the palace.

pp. 121–122   Roehm massacre: Bullock, *Hitler*, pp. 59, 284–307, 667, 774.

———   Bonhoeffer's reaction: recalled in conversation with E. Bethge.

p. 123   Fanö: NRS, pp. 279–296 (letters, speeches, resolutions); IKDB, pp. 85–90 (Dudzus); DB/EB, pp. 431–454.

p. 126   *Cost of Discipleship* (trans. by R. H. Fuller), Macmillan. New York, 1949.

———   *Life Together* (trans. by J. Dobberstein), Harper, New York, 1954.

———   Bonhoeffer's prison thoughts about Finkenwalde: LP, p. 201.

pp. 126–127   Bethge on question of a "conversion": *Bonhoeffer in a World Come of Age*, pp. 79–81; DB/EB, p. 214.

pp. 127–128   Bonhoeffer turns to ultimate for sake of penultimate: TWTF, p. 31 (GS, vol. II, p. 449); *World Come of Age*, p. 52 (Bethge's essay); also "bellicose ghetto" idea in *World Come of Age*, pp. 64–65.

p. 128   "he who severs himself, etc.": TWTF,

pp. 93–94 (whole paper, pp. 75–96, with debate continuing through p. 114; GS reference is vol. II, p. 238); DB/EB, p. 590.

p. 129 "Jews . . . Gregorian chants": *Ethics* (paperback, 1963), pp. 113–114; also quoted in *World Come of Age*, p. 81.

———— "the voice of the dumb": GS, vol. I, p. 42, in a letter to Erwin Sutz; the phrase recurs, though.

p. 130 Zingst: DB/EB, pp. 486–488.

p. 132 Josquin des Prés: DB/EB, p. 488.

———— Finkenwalde arrangements: IKDB, pp. 123–137 and 145–149; NRS, pp. 297–344; TWTF, pp. 29–74 and 259–264; DB/EB, pp. 488–493 and 529–532.

p. 133 confession: DB/EB, pp. 532–533; *Life Together*, pp. 112–113.

p. 134 housekeeping details: IKDB, pp. 107–111 (Zimmermann).

p. 135 rearmament and draft: DB/EB, pp. 494–495.

p. 136 Barth leaves Germany (the issue): Gill, *Some Recent Protestant Political Thinking*, pp. 95–96.

p. 137 Confessing Church made illegal: DB/EB, pp. 564–566.

p. 138 Ruth von Kleist to rescue: IKDB, pp. 114–122 (W. Koch); DB/EB, pp. 502–504.

p. 139 communicants' class: *Bonhoeffer in a World Come of Age* (M. von Wedemeyer-Weller), p. 104; DB/EB, p. 503.

———— buying up the protest: DB/EB, pp. 566–567.

p. 140 one student leaves Finkenwalde: DB/EB, pp. 570–572.

———— grandmother's funeral: VEU, pp. 96–97; DB/EB, p. 574.

pp. 141–143 Swedish birthday trip: TWTF, pp. 51–54; DB/EB, pp. 575–584.

p. 143 dismissal from university: DB/EB, p. 581.

p. 144 Chamby: DB/EB, pp. 619–627.

pp. 144–146 white paper episode: Cochrane, pp. 268–279; DB/EB, pp. 602–607.

p. 175   trip to document genocide: DB/EB, p. 836.

pp. 176–177   U-7 and C. Friedenthal: DB/EB, pp. 838–841; von Schlabrendorff, p. 169.

p. 177   Gen. von Brauchitsch: DB/EB, p. 742.

p. 178   Bonhoeffer offers to kill: DB/EB, p. 843.
          von Dohnanyi and Gestapo: DB/EB, p. 878.

pp. 178–180   Norway: DB/EB, pp. 844–845.

pp. 180–181   third Swiss trip: DB/EB, pp. 845–850.

p. 181   Schacht as "seismograph": DB/EB, p. 855.

pp. 181–183   Sigtuna, Bell, Schönfeld: GS, vol. I, pp. 372–413 (mostly in English); DB/EB, pp. 850–858.

p. 184   Coffin quote: author's recollection.
          Italy: DB/EB, pp. 866–867.
          Schmidhuber: Deutsch, *The Conspiracy Against Hitler*, pp. 116; Manvell and Fraenkel, *The Canaris Conspiracy*, pp. 72–73, 130–136 and 146–147.

p. 185   all the Abwehr officers are described in full and lively detail in the two books just cited.

pp. 185–187   Maria's mother and engagement: DB/EB, pp. 887–888.

p. 187   English signal: DB/EB, p. 863.

p. 188   bombing attempts: Manvell and Fraenkel, pp. 143–146 and 172–175.
          cantata rehearsal: DB/EB, p. 876.

p. 189   birthday party: DB/EB, p. 882 (the photograph comes after page 880).

pp. 189–190   arrest details: DB/EB, p. 882.

p. 196   legend on wall: LP, p. 46.
          prison impressions: DB/EB, p. 897.

p. 197f.   the legal proceedings: Manvell and Fraenkel, threaded through from p. 155 to 223; DB/EB (from which book the first book cited probably has many details), pp. 898–927 (the author was especially aided in unraveling this part of the story by Dr. Berend Wellmann's careful analysis of Dr. Bethge's sequence of events).

p. 201   Tegel: LP, pp. 22, 81–86 and 121–122; DB/EB, pp. 950–953 (see photograph number 34) and 936–940; *Bonhoeffer in a World Come of Age* (essay by Maria von Wedemeyer-Weller), pp. 103–113.

pp. 203–204   Hans to hospital: Manvell and Fraenkel, p. 176 and 178–179; DB/EB, pp. 906–908.

pp. 205–206   von dem Bussche: Manvell and Fraenkel, p. 175; DB/EB, p. 907.

———   Bonhoeffer's 38th birthday: LP, pp. 127–130.

pp. 208–209   the von Hase visit: LP, pp. 188–189.

p. 209   the "man for others": LP, p. 209 ("Outline for a Book"); the phrase was given great currency, of course, by J. A. T. Robinson, *Honest to God*, pp. 64–83.

p. 210   truth quotes: Bonhoeffer's *Ethics*, pp. 326–334.

p. 211   the prayer idea is remembered from Prof. Reinhold Niebuhr's classes and is added here by the author.

p. 212   von Stauffenberg attempt: Fabian von Schlabrendorff, *The Secret War Against Hitler*, Pitman, New York, 1965, pp. 282–291 (and aftermath, pp. 293–302); Joachim Kramarz, *Stauffenberg*, Macmillan, New York, 1967; Manvell and Fraenkel, op. cit., pp. 179–182ff.; same authors, *The July Plot*, Bodley Head, London, 1964.

p. 213   plot to flee: DB/EB, pp. 927–928.

———   Zossen documents: Manvell and Fraenkel, pp. 190–191.

p. 214   Klaus and Ursula: DB/EB, pp. 928–929.

p. 215   the showers: Manvell and Fraenkel, p. 210; DB/EB, p. 1015.

p. 216   attempt to deceive: DB/EB, p. 1010.

p. 217   poem, "Who Am I": LP, p. 197–198.

p. 220   Freisler death: Manvell and Fraenkel, p. 208; DB/EB, pp. 1022–1023.

pp. 221–222   Bonhoeffer birthday and departure to Buchenwald: DB/EB, pp. 1023 and 1026–1028.

pp. 222–223   "principles": Bonhoeffer's *Ethics*, pp. 7–8, 122 and 186.

p. 225   Maria's trip: DB/EB, pp. 1019–1020.

CREDITS

p. 226 food to prisoners: from conversations with Dr. and Mrs. Bethge.

pp. 227–228 trip from Buchenwald to Regensburg: LP, pp. 227–228 (Bethge essay); DB/EB, pp. 1030–1032.

p. 229 sure worst is over; breakdown; LP, p. 229; DB/EB, pp. 1032–1033.

pp. 230–234 Schönberg: LP, pp. 230–232; DB/EB, pp. 1033–1036.

——— "radical" theological developments: LP, pp. 151–202.

p. 235 Bonhoeffer's departure: LP, p. 233; DB/EB, p. 1037; Payne Best, *The Venlo Incident*, Hutchinson, London, 1950, p. 200.

pp. 235–238 the Flossenbürg road: details from a trip made by the author over the same route in the first week of April, 1969; Flossenbürg camp, prison, and cell details worked out at same time.

——— Maria: DB/EB, p. 1041.

p. 239 BBC: DB/EB, pp. 1041–1042; VEU, pp. 220–221.

——— "too political": DB/EB, p. 1042.